Kirwan Rockefeller has written a wonderfully he[...] *to boost their self-confidence. Using a variety of directed guided imagery exercises, Rockefeller encourages readers to grow their confidence in steps that are small enough to manage yet big enough to matter. This book is most highly recommended for anyone beginning or ending a job or relationship and for all junior high school students.*

> —David E. Bresler, Ph.D., L.Ac., president of the Academy for Guided Imagery (www.acadgi.com), founder of the UCLA Pain Control Unit, and former White House Commissioner on Complementary and Alternative Medicine Policy

Henry Ford once said, "Whether you believe you can or can't, you're probably right." Kirwan Rockefeller has made a real contribution with this book, teaching you how to use the remarkable power of your imagination to shift from self-doubt and self-criticism to envisioning, affirming, and encouraging yourself to follow your dreams and make them real. Well-written, easy to follow, and it works!

> —Martin L. Rossman, MD, author of *Guided Imagery for Self-Healing* and *Fighting the Cancer Within*, founder of The Healing Mind (www.thehealingmind.org), and cofounder of the Academy for Guided Imagery. (www.academyforguidedimagery.com)

Given the trend toward self-care in health care, Kirwan Rockefeller's book is a refreshingly useful introduction to the use of imagery for self-awareness, confidence, and resiliency. The guided and multisensory imagery chapters are presented with case vignettes and sample exercises that will greatly enhance the work of coaches, educators, and psychotherapists.

> —Ilene A. Serlin, Ph.D, ADTR, founder and director of Union Street Health Associates, Inc. in San Francisco, CA and series editor of *Mind-Body Medicine: The Art of Whole Person Healthcare*

This clear, concise, user-friendly book combines practical advice with guided-imagery exercises designed to replace helplessness with independence, despair with affirmation, pessimism with assertiveness, and doubt in one's abilities with a reality-based sense of trust that can unleash one's most exciting potential. Rockefeller has based his suggestions on cutting-edge research in the psychology of creativity, management, and guided imagery. The results build a bridge between attitudes and behaviors that have the potential of leading the reader to lifelong changes in both.

> —Stanley Krippner, Ph.D., coeditor of *The Varieties of Anomalous Experience* and executive faculty member at the Saybrook Graduate School and Research Center in San Francisco, CA

Having taught imagery to healthcare professionals and having used it as a therapeutic modality in my private practice for more than twenty years, I can testify to the power of imagery to build confidence. Kirwan Rockefeller has created a clear, step-by-step journey for anyone of any age to follow. I particularly like his use of imagery scripts, vision boards, and journaling exercises. These form a wonderful combination that not only builds confidence but stirs creativity. Rockefeller's book speaks to the head and the heart to help people confidently live their life to the fullest.

> —Judith Westerfield, MA, marriage and family therapist and executive faculty member at the Academy for Guided Imagery in Laguna Niguel, CA

Visualize Confidence

how to use guided imagery to overcome self-doubt

kirwan rockefeller, ph.d.

New Harbinger Publications, Inc.

Guided Imagery Exercise 1 in Introduction is from the book *Guided Imagery for Self-Healing.* Copyright ©2000 by Martin L. Rossman. Reprinted with permission of HJ Kramer/New World Library, Novato, CA. www.newworldlibrary.com.

Awareness Exercise 13 is reprinted with permission of New Harbinger Publications. *What's Right with Me*, copyright ©Carlene DeRoo and Carolyn DeRoo. www.newharbinger.com.

Guided Imagery Exercise 6 is reprinted with permission of New Harbinger Publications. *Five Good Minutes*, copyright ©Jeffrey Brantley and Wendy Millstine. www.newharbinger.com.

"Visualizing," copyright © Dan Brodsky-Chenfeld and Jack Jeffries, from www.dropzone.com, appears with permission of the authors.

Distributed in Canada by Raincoast Books

Library of Congress Cataloging-in-Publication Data

Rockefeller, Kirwan.
  Visualize confidence : how to use guided imagery to overcome self-doubt / Kirwan Rockefeller.
    p. cm.
  Includes bibliographical references.
  ISBN-13: 978-1-57224-494-8
  ISBN-10: 1-57224-494-1
  1. Imagery (Psychology) 2. Visualization. 3. Self-confidence. I. Title.
BF367.R634 2007
153.3'2--dc22

                           2006102708

09   08   07
10   9   8   7   6   5   4   3   2   1
First printing

To Ruth and C. K., Mom and Dad
"The best is yet to be."

contents

foreword

In 1975, I was invited to do research on the cancer patients in groups held by Carl and Stephanie Simonton in Fort Worth, Texas. This work was a time outside of time—an epiphany—when I knew that my life would never again be the same. The Simontons' practices were novel; they were working with patients, all diagnosed with terminal or stage IV cancer, who chose to fight for a return to health by intensely examining their lives and making radical changes. Imagery was an important part of the therapy, and the patients were guided through exercises in which they envisioned their cancer cells being attacked by their immune defenses. I was hooked. Here was the drama of being human; priorities were set, and what was of value to them rose like cream to the top of their concerns, while what was trivial and of little importance settled to the bottom.

In 1999, I joined Jim Gordon's group from the Center for Mind/ Body medicine on a mission to the refugee camps in Macedonia at the onset of the war in Kosovo. Ethic Albanians were fleeing their own country, thousands crossing the border every day. At first, I thought the refuges would need "real medicine," like assistance with wounds and childbirth. Not so. What they needed, instead, was medicine for their hearts and souls. We taught them imagery and meditation in several forms. They were offered strategies for stress management and an opportunity to express their anguish and fears. Imagery was present even in the midst of war.

Two years later, a group of spouses and other family members of the brave New York firefighters who died on 9/11 met at a retreat in the Catskill Mountains. Again, I was allowed to participate. Again I witnessed people in the throes of being human, people who sought meaning in the horrible acts of terrorism and solace in a healing community. Here, imagery was also a vital part of individual and group healing.

In 1999, within days of my diagnosis of ocular melanoma, healing circles had formed on my behalf all over the globe. Symbols and images of healing arrived daily in the mail; pictures of saints and healers, icons, and uplifting books and notes. Once more, imagery was present all around me. I remain convinced today that the healing circles, the symbols and images sent to me, as well as those images within me were the reason I had the unusual remission. They were my main medicine.

So, what is medicine, anyway? What is imagery and why is it important? As I wrote in the book *Rituals of Healing: Using Imagery for Health and Wellness* (1994) with colleagues Barbara Dossey and Leslie Kolkmeier, imagery, the powerful expression of the imagination, is the basis for self-generated healing and symbolizes what cannot be seen or experienced directly. Albert Einstein, who claimed that imagination is more important than knowledge, is said to have first recognized the distortion of time and space by imagining himself riding on a ray, traveling at the speed of light.

Kirwan Rockefeller, a student of mine at Saybrook Graduate School and Research Center, is a fine scholar and sensitive to all levels of humanity. Under my guidance, Dr. Rockefeller received one of the highest awards given by Saybrook Institute in 1993, the Thuss Award for Academic Excellence, for his doctoral candidacy essay,

"Psychoneuroimmunology and Biopsychosocial Cofactors of HIV-Spectrum Disease and Long-Term Survivors." He is quite knowledgeable about using guided imagery, rituals, and other integrative modalities for health and well-being.

This book will teach you valuable and time-proven skills and techniques for tapping into your imagination to develop self-confidence. These guided imagery skills will help you find your individual strengths and resources to live an empowered and assured life.

—Jeanne Achterberg, Ph.D.
Executive Faculty
Saybrook Graduate School & Research Center
San Francisco, California

acknowledgments

I'd like to extend my deepest appreciation to the staff of New Harbinger Publications, who have supported this book from the time it was but a faint image in my mind. In particular, I thank Matthew McKay, Ph.D., Tesilya Hanauer, Heather Mitchener, Carole Honeychurch, and Karen O'Donnell Stein. Their vision, expertise, and encouragement have been invaluable. I couldn't have done it without them.

Thanks go to my teachers and mentors, Jeanne Achterberg, Ph.D.; David Bresler, Ph.D.; Stanley Krippner, Ph.D.; David Lukoff, Ph.D.; Martin Rossman, MD; Ilene Serlin, Ph.D.; Dennis Jaffe, Ph.D.; and all my colleagues at Saybrook Graduate School and Research Center in San Francisco. I am fortunate to have learned from their vast knowledge and am grateful for their guidance. In addition, special thanks go to my colleagues at the University of California, Irvine, particularly Gary Matkin, Ph.D., dean, and Jane Welgan, Ed.D., associate dean, for their steadfast support.

I'd like to thank my family for their continued patience over the years. I'm sure my parents, C. K. and Ruth, and my sisters, Patricia and Carolyn, never imagined that an early childhood event would have such a profound effect on and lasting motivation for my growth. I thank them for their love. Finally, I'd like to thank my partner, Kirk Snyder, an accomplished professional writer in his own right, who offered a treasure trove of advice and encouragement.

introduction

"Even the wildest dreams have to start someplace. Allow
yourself the time and space to let your mind wander and
your imagination fly. . . . You must be a believer before you
can be an achiever." —Oprah Winfrey

Confidence is a tricky thing. One moment you feel on top of the
world, able to accomplish all your hopes and dreams, and the
next minute you feel your knees buckle—you become tongue-tied
and are unable to even say hello. How can confidence be so strong
one moment and then so fleeting and elusive the next? What magic
ingredients do superconfident people possess that make them appear
unflappable? And, most important, you ask, "How can I become more
confident and self-assured in life?"

Real Confidence: What It Is and What It Isn't

Like a strong tree that bends in hurricane-force winds, real confidence is rooted in what your inherent abilities are, and it is firmly grounded in the core belief that you do have the skills to act with certainty and assurance. Often marked by a feeling of relaxed coolness, real confidence gives you freedom from embarrassment, and the conviction that "I *can* do it!" Real confidence, which could also be called faith in yourself, is without haughtiness or conceit; it is the recognition that you are adequate, capable, and competent and have the resources to accomplish the tasks at hand.

Real confidence isn't something on the outside that you need to acquire, a specific quality of life in the distant future, or the expectation of reaching an unrealistic goal without applying yourself. It's important to know that real confidence isn't arrogant, aggressive, or stubborn. It doesn't require brute willpower, or sheer force of personality. Neither is real confidence manipulative, controlling of others, or selfish. And, most certainly, real self-confidence isn't about making others yield to your demands or making them feel inferior while they cower beneath your supremacy.

YOURS TO RECLAIM

When nurtured from childhood, real confidence gives you a solid foundation for independence. When your parents or caretakers instill self-reliance in you, even when you make mistakes, you grow up knowing you can trust yourself.

But many of us struggle to reclaim confidence as our natural birthright. Even if you were vulnerable in childhood when your basic beliefs were formed, with each passing day you have the opportunity to reclaim your confidence and banish deceptive feelings of helplessness. Your feelings of helplessness can be replaced with the conviction that you have what it takes and that you can create positive growth in your life.

Real confidence is within you at all times. It's always been there; it's just been misplaced, forgotten, or trampled upon. Real confidence is your natural birthright. What makes this book unique is that it shows how you can use guided imagery and the power of your own imagination to feel confident.

A Picture Is Worth a Thousand Words

Have you ever remodeled a room? Planned a vacation? Have you ever applied for a new job, prepared to make a speech, or worried about a difficult conversation in the future? Any activity that requires you to look ahead into the future or plan ahead begins with a picture in your mind, or an image.

Beliefs, feelings, attitudes, and ideas are represented and deeply rooted in imagery. Imagery can be thought of initially as pictures in your mind; yet imagery is so much more than that. Imagery is a full sensory experience made of thoughts that you can see, feel, hear, taste, and smell. Imagery can be about events that have happened in the past or have yet to happen. Rich in symbols, imagery tells us how we see ourselves, how we see others, and how we plan for the future. Imagery is a window into your inner world—the world of dreams, daydreams, fantasies, and your creative imagination. Imagery is also a reflection of your outer world, the world of self-image and confidence. This book will help you focus the power of your creative imagination by using your natural ability to imagine to gain new levels of confidence.

NEGATIVE IMAGERY

Many of the images we hold in our minds, such as pleasant memories, a beautiful sunset, a prayer or meditation, or an upcoming summer vacation, are positive and life affirming. However, most of the time the images we play over and over in our minds are fearful, worrisome, and full of self-doubt. These are the images that undermine our confidence.

Let's say you've been asked to give a new marketing-strategy presentation to senior management at work. As you begin preparing for this event, you automatically remember presenting your sixth-grade book report. Your body starts to tense up, your heart begins to race, your palms begin to sweat, your muscles tighten—and now, instead of feeling confident, you're anxious and afraid. The negative imagery has put you in a bad mood and you begin to project all the things that could go wrong. You start to ruminate on a variety of negative thoughts and images: "Will the boss be pleased? Will I embarrass myself in front of all my colleagues? What if I stutter? What if I sweat? I can't handle this!" Your confidence flies out the window as a cascade of activity begins in your brain, clouding your mind and making your body a hodgepodge of muscle tension, aches, and pains. And your confidence tanks.

Not a positive image, is it?

POSITIVE IMAGERY

Now, let's imagine you've spent years dreaming about going to Italy. You've watched all the travel and history shows on television about Rome and the Renaissance, and your favorite food is spaghetti. In your mind's eye, you can see yourself cruising along the Mediterranean or floating down Venice's Grand Canal in a gondola, your fingers gently skimming the cool water. You daydream about standing in the Sistine Chapel imagining Michelangelo maneuvering the heights on scaffolding. You're tasting wine in Tuscany and smelling the delicious aroma of food being prepared in a little out-of-the-way neighborhood restaurant. You picture yourself flying across the ocean and landing in another world, thinking, "Hey, I'm finally here; this is a dream come true!"

Now this is a positive image!

THE MIND IS A POWERFUL ALLY

Your mind responds equally to both negative and positive images. It doesn't matter what you're imagining, because your mind and body don't know the difference. This process of responding equally to both negative and positive imagery is the basis of your creative imagination. It's this very basic process that you'll learn to harness by reading this book.

In today's Western world, the power of the imagination isn't always valued, except in specific artistic endeavors. Our culture often tends to downplay it as insignificant or frivolous and not having much to do with day-to-day life. Many people dismiss imagination with an "it's all in your head" attitude, as if this were a bad thing. We've forgotten or misplaced the awareness that creative imagination opens our souls and minds to new possibilities and opportunities not available to the cognitive, rational mind.

When you learn to focus your creative imagination, you'll have at your disposal a powerful ally. Your creative imagination is a partner available to you at any time and any place to help you turn your dreams into reality and gain confidence. With focus and learning to utilize this power, you'll be able to live free from self-doubt and become the person you've always wanted to be.

In his bestseller *The 7 Habits of Highly Effective People* (2004), Stephen Covey suggests that when you use the power of your creative imagination you align with your deepest values in life, because the creative imagination is personal, positive, visual, and emotional. And don't you deserve to live the best life possible, free from self-doubt? Of course you do! There's no need to let self-doubt stop you cold, time and time again.

What Is Self-Doubt?

Merriam-Webster's Collegiate Dictionary defines doubt as "uncertainty of belief or opinion that often interferes with decision-making; . . . a state of affairs giving rise to uncertainty, hesitation, or suspense . . . a lack of confidence" (2003, 375). In individuals, self-doubt is the belief that we can't trust ourselves and don't have what it takes to be successful. In fact, self-doubt doesn't merely interfere; it kidnaps your beliefs and behavior! Self-doubt makes you beat yourself up with a torrent of negative self-talk and recriminations, such as "You don't measure up and won't ever measure up." When self-doubt captures your life force it can lead to a variety of physical and psychological ailments, including depression, headaches, muscle tension, cold sweats, hyperventilation, anxiety, insomnia, ulcers, a host of gastrointestinal problems, and feelings of victimization.

Self-doubt thrives on fear: fear of the unknown, fear of saying no to others, fear of not being liked, fear of change, fear of failure, and, yes, even fear of success. When the exasperating voice of self-doubt does its job, your self-confidence, self-esteem, and self-reliance deflate like a burst balloon, and fearful imagery controls your past, present, and future. "Why," you ask, "am I so afraid?"

F.E.A.R.

Fear is a natural, healthy, and useful emotion. It is the unpleasant feeling you have when you perceive danger in your environment, whether real or imagined. Studied in thousands of research investigations, it is the underlying cause of the well-known "fight or flight" response to danger. When fear hits the pit of your stomach, you know to either take a stand and fight or to flee to safety. As a belief mechanism, fear is one of the most basic of human emotions.

Healthy fear is a warning system. For thousands of years, fear has alerted us to the need to take action, and certainly to evaluate what is in front of us. For example, suppose you were asked to cross the Grand Canyon on a rickety wooden bridge spanning the enormous cavern. Your fear in this situation might be a very good protective mechanism, causing you to check out the structure, question the bridge's sturdiness, and, after evaluating the potential for injury, decide whether to walk across the bridge.

Fear can range from distrust to dread and fright, to paranoia and terror. While distrust is a mild form of fear, abject terror can literally frighten you to death. Two phrases sum up the real response to fear: "false evidence appearing real" and "forget everything and run."

Time and again I've seen fear and fear-based imagery stop people dead in their tracks. I've witnessed strong, capable people freeze up, unable to move forward in life, accomplish their goals, and realize long-held dreams. All too often these goals and dreams remain incomplete while people accept false evidence appearing real. Or, in the face of self-doubt, they drop everything and run.

But, it doesn't have to be like this. While you can't ever completely rid yourself of fear, nor would you actually want to, you can learn to use it to your advantage as you work to build confidence. You deserve and can have a confident life.

Why I Wrote This Book

As a university educator, I've worked with hundreds of men and women who are searching for confidence and more fulfilling, creatively charged lives. Rarely do people come to me and say, "You know, I wish I could spend more time working at my boring office job," or "I wish I could be filled with more self-doubt." Instead, people say, "I want to be more confident, more creative, more alive, and more aware. I want to live the life I've always imagined for myself!" But the habitual feelings and images that have stuck in their minds for years don't support confident risk taking.

Do you want to think outside the box? Do you want to be more confident and creative and live the life you've imagined for yourself?

If so, this book is for you. Banishing self-doubt from your life and living with confidence is as simple as becoming aware of the negative and positive imagery in your mind and how it affects your beliefs, attitudes, and behavior. Using the tools of guided imagery, you can direct the very thoughts and images in your mind so that you can reach new levels of motivation and success. And it all begins with an image in your mind.

Imagery is everywhere. We are visual and sensory people who instinctively know that a picture is worth a thousand words. All you have to do is look around and see the millions of images that bombard us daily: magazines, books, billboards, advertisements, commercials, movies, television, and newspapers. In addition, there are literally thousands of images running around in your mind—images that you may not even be consciously aware of. These images dictate how you feel and act. But, more important, these images can be changed by the practical application of guided imagery tools.

I wrote this book to help you learn how to use guided imagery to overcome self-doubt and live a confident life. My own life has been a grand training ground for the power of creative imagination, and I've seen the effects of these simple tools on countless lives.

About the Author

I'm hearing impaired and was raised in a hearing impaired and deaf family. So, ever since I was a small boy I've been drawn to imagery and the power of the imagination. I discovered at an early age that the cliché is true: when one sense (in my case, hearing) is compromised, the other senses become sharper. Instinctively drawn to pictures, colors, textures, patterns, and shapes, I perceived how these elements were reflective of, and in relationship with, the energy that swirled around me in the world. I could intuitively interpret visual and feeling clues, smells, tastes, and the movements of everything and everyone around me. I could understand them within a larger context of relationships and behavior.

My favorite childhood pastime was building model airplanes. I could build a model merely by looking at the photograph or drawing on the front of the box. Having no need for directions, I could see in my mind how all the parts fit together. Likewise, I was mesmerized by magazines, television, and movies. In every picture I saw, I was enthralled by the symbols, patterns, and elements of design used to convey meaning.

When my family bought our first color television set in the mid-1960s, I discovered how this big, boxy console that opened up a world of color could bring thousands of images into our home and into my mind. My sensory perceptions and intuition became even more finely honed, as did my ability to know what was being conveyed nonverbally by a simple gesture, tone of voice, or movement—all pictures spoke to me with a thousand words. I learned that imagery and my imagination were powerful forces in the world.

I began my formal college education in art history and theater. In art history I studied imagery and symbolism from ancient times to the modern era. I learned how imagery conveyed deep meaning for cultures around the globe, and how these images and symbols were ingrained historically, socially, and politically within a personal and collective context. In theater I learned how imagery could come alive and how the purposeful intention of an actor could paint an emotional scene for an entire audience.

Quite by accident, one day in the late 1970s I picked up a small book entitled *Creative Visualization*, written by Shatki Gawain (1978, 2002). Immediately I realized that the process Shatki talked about was something I had been doing quite instinctively all my life. This book prompted me to learn more about the mechanisms at work in creative visualization. My path eventually took me to Los Angeles, where I became employed at Universal Studios. Needless to say, working in one of the world's best-known imagery factories, which created "moving pictures," was a priceless experience. Here, I observed the worldwide influence of imagery with color, sound, light, and sensory stimulation within stories projected onto a silver screen one hundred feet tall.

I then learned about the dynamic work of Jeanne Achterberg, David Bresler, Martin Rossman, and Stanley Krippner. Their work matched my own interests, including imagery, symbolism, personal mythology, health, and wellness, which subsequently led me to pursue doctoral studies in psychology and human science. I surveyed the many ways in which humans use imagery to define and understand their worlds. I was intrigued with the macrocosm of worldwide motion-picture imagery to the microcosm of individual imagery that bridges the mind and the body. With Jeanne Achterberg I studied psychoneuro-immunology (PNI), the science of the interactions between the mind (*psycho-*), the brain (*neuro-*), behavior, and the immune system. The term "psychoneuroimmunology" was originally coined by Robert Ader and Nicholas Cohen in 1975 at the University of Rochester. Since that time PNI research has demonstrated a dramatic interrelationship between the body and the mind using imagery. From the work of David Bresler and Martin Rossman I learned about Interactive Guided Imagery and the power of imagery insight turned into action. Along the way, my interactions with hundreds of experts, students, and clients have brought me to the point where I can now share with you the strategies and tools of using guided imagery to overcome self-doubt.

How to Use This Book

You were born with superb confidence and the ability to be the artist of your own life. Yet over the years you may have lost your way, misplaced your confidence, or through the school of hard knocks had your confidence severely bruised. If so, not to worry. This book will help you rediscover your authentic confidence.

You can read this book's chapters in any order you wish, but it's best to follow the chapters in sequence, because they build upon one another. Your journey in visualizing confidence will begin with an assessment of your current confidence level (chapter 1). Next you'll identify the fundamentals of guided imagery (chapter 2), reclaim your natural confidence (chapter 3), and choose what to focus on (chapter 4). You'll learn and practice several simple imagery techniques along the way. You'll then discover how small changes can make a big impact (chapter 5), practice new positive behavior (chapter 6), and learn to focus on what's right and celebrate yourself (chapter 7). You'll finish up by putting it all together and identifying a new self-image for living confidently (chapter 8).

THE EXERCISES IN THIS BOOK

Don't just read this book; allow yourself to experience it with the full power of your imagination and all your senses. You might find unexpected surprises as you learn new skills. Be open-minded and approach the exercises with curiosity, asking yourself, "I wonder what I'll learn from this?" Working with the exercises in this book will offer you a positive and enjoyable journey.

To get the most benefits from this book, plan on fully integrating all the exercises into your life. In chapter 4 you'll decide on the most important confidence goal that you wish to accomplish. When you pick a goal, stick with it, and work on one goal at a time. Below are some examples of confidence goals:

- Going to a party and talking to someone new when you feel shy

- Asking the boss for a raise

- Dating again after a divorce

- Making a career change

- Speaking in public

- Going on a job interview

- Going back to school

- Taking initiative when you're filled with self-doubt

- Voicing your opinion when you feel small

- Caring less about what others think

- Standing up for yourself

- Having better sex

- Delivering difficult news to someone

- Feeling better about your body

- Facing the prospect of surgery

- Starting a new chapter in your life

A Daily Practice: Repetition and Consistency

The keys to using guided imagery to build your self-confidence are repetition and consistency. As you read through this book, I recommend you set aside twenty to thirty minutes each day to read the chapters and do the exercises, ideally at the same time every day. Create a daily practice for yourself; it doesn't matter when you do use imagery, as long as you are consistent each and every day. With daily practice you'll find yourself becoming calmer, more centered, and more relaxed. Getting into the habit of using the exercises will incrementally build your level of confidence.

Make sure you have uninterrupted time to devote to the exercises. After the kids have gone to school or to bed may be a good time. Create a small sanctuary for yourself and let the answering machine pick up phone calls. This is your time. This is a gift you can give yourself.

Do all of the exercises at least once. Some may work well for you, and others perhaps not as well; that's okay. But it's important to commit to trying all of them. Be kind to yourself and give yourself permission to be open to new ways of thinking and acting.

Purchase a nice notebook to use with this book. I particularly like bound sketch pads sold at art-supply stores, special pens of different colors, and highlighters. Your self-confidence notebook will become a trusted companion. Throughout your journey you may even find yourself embellishing it with colorful postcards, magazine clippings, photographs, stories, or poetry.

A word of caution: if you share this notebook and its exercises with others, you may find that some people aren't entirely supportive. Recognize that they may not want to support your becoming a self-confident person. Perhaps they fear that a change in you will mean you won't need them anymore. If this happens, don't push yourself to make major decisions in your life immediately. Give new thoughts, feelings, images, and behavior a bit of time to mature. Safeguard your new confidence as if it were a small spring seedling that needed protection. Work at your own pace, and remember to take it easy.

Insight Leads to Action

The exercises in this book, both the guided imagery and the awareness exercises, are designed to provide you, first and foremost, with insight. New insight will propel you toward new self-knowledge. This new self-knowledge will form the basis of your positive growth and enhance your level of self-confidence. Your new insights and self-knowledge will lead you to new perceptions. New perceptions will, in turn, encourage you to explore new options, and new options always mean new behaviors. Practicing new behaviors, as well as new ways of thinking and being, will propel you to make decisions differently than you have done in the past. Like a broken record, or a defective CD that skips all the time, we tend to do the same thing over and over, yet we expect new results. Of this I'm certain: if you want new results, you must act in new ways!

Acting in new ways with new behavior will support you as you explore new options. Exploring new options ultimately creates new results. And who among us doesn't want a new result? In fact, isn't that why you picked up this book in the first place? You want a new result that will allow you to overcome your self-doubt and replace it with new and improved self-confidence. This entire process will help you develop healthy and vital confidence!

The spiral diagram below shows how using guided imagery works to build self-confidence.

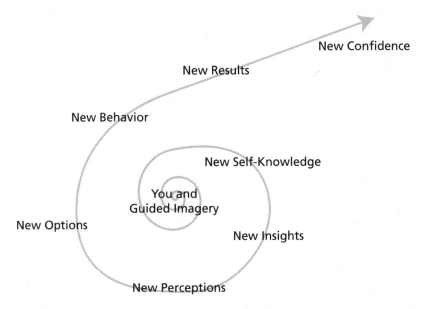

Above all, this will be an empowering journey for you. There's no need to worry about struggle or pain along the way. Working with imagery is a natural and easy way to visualize new levels of confidence.

Working with a Therapist

Therapists and doctors can be wonderful sources of support as you come across new perspectives and new self-images in your journey. If you're working with a psychotherapist, be sure to share this book and your process with him or her. If you're under a doctor's care, by all means share this book with that person too. Anything that helps you become the confident person you aspire to be can only be good.

USING GUIDED IMAGERY SCRIPTS

In this book you'll notice guided imagery directions, called *scripts*, which are simply road maps to working with the exercises. There are several effective ways in which you can use these scripts. If possible, try out several methods to find the one that works best for you. For example, you can ask a friend to read the guided imagery script out loud, speaking clearly and calmly, pausing for five to ten seconds between each step. Remember, there's no need to rush through this process; it is designed to be comforting and relaxing. Alternatively, try reading it into an audio recorder and then playing it back, listening to your own familiar voice. Or you can familiarize yourself with the script until you know it by heart, allowing you to guide yourself through the exercise without any audio prompts.

If you decide to use an audio recorder, do not play the recording while driving a car or operating any type of machinery. You want to be in a quiet space where you won't be interrupted. Most important, remember to go slowly, and be gentle with yourself.

After you finish a guided imagery exercise, give yourself plenty of time to ponder the images, feelings, and sensations that come up for you. Don't immediately jump up and start doing errands or chores. Sit quietly as the sensations and thoughts come to you, and make notes of the images and symbols that arise in your consciousness in your journal. You may find yourself writing a poem or engaging in some simple ritual, like drinking cool, fresh lemon water, or blowing out a candle. The images, feelings, insights, thoughts, and symbols that arise during this and all other exercises in this book are coming from your own mind, from the wisdom of your own psyche. It can feel dreamlike and hazy and will vanish too quickly if you don't take the time to sit, ponder, and record it in some way. Don't evaluate, judge, or dismiss your experience as silly and a waste of time.

These simple and easy techniques have had a tremendous impact on many people's lives. While this book doesn't promise to instantly solve all your problems in life, it does promise the chance for a fresh, new approach: living free of self-doubt and filled with new confidence.

Now, let's get started with a simple guided imagery script to jump-start your imaginative abilities.

A FIRST IMAGERY EXPERIENCE

The exercise below, "Exploring Your Imagery Abilities," was created by Martin Rossman (2000), a physician and cofounder, with David Bresler, of the Academy for Guided Imagery. It is reproduced here with his permission from his book *Guided Imagery for Self-Healing*.

Position yourself comfortably, either lying down or sitting, and loosen any tight clothing. Create a quiet place where you won't be disturbed for the next twenty to thirty minutes. It's okay to move or shift your body position at any time to become more comfortable. With your eyes closed, you're ready to begin.

Guided Imagery Exercise #1 ─────────────

Begin by getting comfortable where you are . . . let yourself breathe easily and comfortably . . . take a couple of slow, deep breaths and let the out breath be a real letting-go kind of breath . . . just begin to let go of any unnecessary tension or discomfort . . . as you relax allow your eyes to close and begin to focus inside. . . .

As I ask you to imagine a variety of things, allow yourself to observe what happens for you . . . remember, there is no right or wrong way to imagine these things . . . just notice what it's like for you . . . that's your only responsibility now . . . noticing what it's like. . . .

Imagine a triangle . . . any type of triangle will do . . . you may imagine you see it on a screen, like a movie or television screen, or you may imagine it in your mind . . . just notice which is easier for you . . . notice what type of triangle you see . . . perhaps there is more than one . . . notice if the image is steady and vivid, or if it comes and goes, or changes as you watch it . . . remember, it doesn't really matter how you imagine it . . . just stay relaxed and observe what is happening. . . .

If you'd like the image to be clearer or more vivid, imagine you have a set of controls like you do on your TV set and experiment with them until the image is the way you want it . . . or just take a couple of deep breaths and relax more deeply as you let them go, letting the image become clearer as you do . . . notice how these techniques work for you. . . .

Now let the image go . . . and let a square form in your mind's eye or on your mental screen . . . any kind of square is fine . . . just notice what it's like as you continue to observe it . . . now let that image fade and imagine a circle . . . notice how big or small it is, and how round . . . let the circle be yellow . . . a bright yellow circle . . . notice if it helps you to think of the sun or a yellow lemon . . . let the yellow fade and imagine the circle is red . . . like an apple or something red that's familiar to you . . . now let that go and imagine the circle is blue . . . like the sky or the ocean . . . let the circle become three-dimensional and form a sphere . . . and let the sphere begin to rotate slowly . . . see it rotating and let it become a globe, spinning in space, as if you were looking at the earth from outer space. . . .

Now come back to earth . . . imagine you are in the country, and it's wintertime . . . you are walking through the freshly fallen snow and can hear and feel it crunch beneath your boots . . . the air is cold and crisp, and you can see your breath as you exhale . . . in the distance a church bell is pealing . . . and somewhere a radio is playing "Jingle Bells" . . . notice what that sounds like. . . .

Now let that image fade and imagine instead you are on a beautiful warm tropical beach . . . the sky is blue, and the sun is bright and warm on your skin . . . the sand is warm beneath your feet . . . the ocean is vast, and the waves roll to the shore one after the other in a timeless, tireless rhythm . . . you can hear the sound of the waves breaking, advancing, and retreating on the sand . . . imagine that you walk down toward the water, feeling the sand becoming hotter underneath your feet . . . you may begin to walk a little more quickly as it becomes hotter and hotter . . . as you reach the water line where the water has washed and cooled the sand and you feel the relief of the cool wetness on the soles of your feet as you walk a little way into the cool swirling water, it washes around your ankles, and as it retreats, it draws away some of the sand beneath your feet . . . the movement of the sand and water feels good beneath you. . . .

Now let that image go . . . and imagine you are in a room from your childhood—a room where you had some good experiences . . . notice where you are . . . and what you see there . . . notice what sounds you hear there . . . and perhaps an odor or aroma that's special to that place . . . notice how it feels to be there. . . .

Let that image go . . . and imagine the aroma of fresh-ground coffee . . . now imagine there's a plate of your favorite food in front of you, beautifully prepared from the freshest ingredients . . . you lean over and inhale the aroma . . . then taste it . . . notice what it's like as you taste it, chew it . . . and swallow. . . .

Let that go . . . and imagine you are walking along the path in the forest . . . it's a beautiful day . . . and you meet someone friendly on the path . . . you stop to have a brief conversation with this person . . . notice who you meet and what you talk about . . . notice how you communicate with one another. . . .

If there are any loose ends, or if you want to continue this talk, arrange with the imaginary person to meet again at a later time. . . .

Now let that go . . . and recall some time you felt very much at peace with yourself . . . a time when you felt very peaceful, very centered, and calm . . . imagine it as if it were happening right now . . . notice where you are . . . and who you're with . . . what you're doing . . . notice your posture . . . and your face . . . your voice . . . especially notice the feelings of peacefulness and centeredness in you . . . notice where you feel these qualities, and let them be there . . . let them begin to grow in you . . . let them amplify and expand, filling your whole body with feelings of peacefulness and calm . . . let the feelings overflow your body to fill the space around you . . . so that all of you is bathed in this peacefulness. . . .

Now slowly let yourself begin to become aware of the room . . . and let yourself become awake and alert, bringing back with you any feeling of peacefulness you may have experienced . . . remember what was of interest or importance to you, and take some time to write about it.

Debriefing Your First Experience

Did you find it easy to experience the different colors, shapes, and scenes? What comes to mind as you think and write about your first imagery encounter? Were you able to relax and adjust the images easily?

Were you able to feel peaceful, restful, and calm? If you noticed any changes, then your body and mind were responding to the natural language of imagery. If not, don't worry; imagery is a skill like any other and with practice you'll find yourself becoming more accomplished.

The Big Picture

This book uses the natural mind-and-body connection of guided imagery that is already in your possession. Focusing the pictures in your mind and connecting them with your attitudes, beliefs, and behavior will help you overcome self-doubt. You have the power to change the imagery in your mind from negative, self-limiting, and defeating images to those that create self-confidence.

You deserve to be self-confident, happy, and prosperous. I wish you well in your journey toward living life confidently.

1

stop self-doubt from stopping you cold

"Only as high as I reach can I grow, only as far as I seek can I go, only as deep as I look can I see, only as much as I dream can I be." —Karen Ravn

Before you can move directly to learning guided imagery techniques to banish self-doubt from your life, let's start with a simple quiz. No need for test anxiety here; this is just a way to identify your starting point. The results of this quiz will be very helpful to you as you progress in this book.

Self-Confidence Quiz

Read through the following twenty questions and let yourself respond naturally and quickly. Try not to think about the questions too much. Instead, go with your initial response, which is always the most accurate. Answer each question using a scale of 1 to 5, with 1 meaning rarely, 2 meaning occasionally, 3 meaning about half of the time, 4 meaning often, and 5 meaning almost all of the time.

I enjoy taking risks and regularly do so. _1 2 3_

I believe I can do anything I put my mind to. _3 4 4_

I seek out new challenges. _1 3 3_

I'm okay if my performance is not perfect all the time. _3 3 4_

I know myself well: strengths, weaknesses, talents, skills, and priorities. _4 4 4_

I'm the person I've always wanted to be. _2 3 4_

I'm comfortable with my actions and don't get embarrassed. _3 4 5_

I thrive on change. _1 3 3_

I have the power to make my dreams come true. _3 4 4_

I always feel self-confident. _3 3 4_

The past is over and I quickly let go of old hurts. _3 3 3_

I do what I feel is right and don't worry about what other people will think. _3 3 3_

I sleep well and don't wake up at night replaying events in my head. _4 4 3_

I love trying new things and don't care if I look foolish. _3 3 4_

I'm just fine the way I am. _2 3 4_

I feel okay when I say no. _1 2 8_

I feel poised and in control when I'm in new situations. _2_ _33_

The best is yet to be. _4 4 5_

I take good care of myself: I eat a healthy diet, exercise, monitor my stress level, and get enough sleep. _4 3 4_

I trust myself to say and do the right things. _2 2 3_

SCORING YOUR SELF-CONFIDENCE QUIZ

Now, add up all your points to determine your total score. Write your score below.

Total score: _52 63 75_

Score of 30 to 59: Congratulations on picking up this book! Your confidence level is low and you'll find many useful tools as we continue.

Score of 60 to 69: You have average confidence already, but it could use some improvement. Keep reading!

Score of 70 to 100: You have strong confidence! But keep reading. This book can help you become even more dynamic.

Visualization and Guided Imagery for Self-Confidence

It's estimated that more than one hundred thousand thoughts and/or images flash through the average person's mind every day. At least half of these thoughts may be self-doubting, negative, or anxiety producing. Experiencing these negative thoughts robs you of the thrill of exploring, discovering new things, meeting new people, and visiting new places. You're left feeling overwhelmed and unable to handle whatever is in front of you. If unchecked, this steady diet of self-doubt, worry, and anxiety affects the very core of who you are: your perceptions of the world, your beliefs about yourself, your moods, and your very health.

Visualization: A Natural Process

Visualization is a natural process that allows you to see pictures in your mind. Visualization is as easy as closing your eyes, imagining you're sitting in a movie theater, and watching the scenes of your life play out on the screen. The pictures you see in your mind can depict actual things in your waking life or things not actually present—in other words, things you want to take place.

Thousands of years ago, early humans painted pictures of the animals they were hunting on the walls of their cave homes. These primitive people might have sat with these paintings, performed small rituals, and allowed the feelings evoked by the paintings to wash over them. They were then able to walk out of their caves full of the confidence and strength necessary for successful hunting. The act of creating the pictures and focusing on them in their mind's eye must have empowered them in amazing and seemingly mystical ways.

Many people, however, don't see these types of pictures in their heads. Research studies tell us that 25 percent of the population do not "see things in their minds, but they use other senses in imagery quite effectively" (Achterberg, Dossey, and Kolkmeier 1994, 38). For these people, guided imagery is the perfect means to tap into the power of their mind's eye to create positive change.

GUIDED IMAGERY: USING ALL YOUR SENSES

Guided imagery is a natural mental thought process that uses sensory information in an unforced, free-flowing way. Actors, athletes, and businesspeople all use mental imagery rehearsals to envision successful performances or to set goals. To use this internally driven technique, you simply close your eyes, take a few deep relaxing breaths, and follow a script to imagine your desired goals. Usually the script is read out loud by a trained therapist in person, but an audio recording can also be used. The use of a script is what makes this technique "guided." With this technique, you have the opportunity to tap into multiple senses and multiple ways of knowing. Your senses will help you feel, on a deep, meaningful level, the self-confidence you've always wanted. Using guided imagery, you can see, hear, smell, taste, and fully sense with your body the feeling you are seeking.

Using powerful brain scanning technology, scientists have recorded the activity that takes place in the brain when we're using visualization and guided imagery. We know that when people visualize or imagine using various senses, the parts of their brains involved with those senses become active. What this means is that the body and the brain don't know the difference between imagined events and real events. The body and the mind are integrally connected.

Guided imagery is an opening for a two-way communication process—a conversation, a dialogue. It acts as a vehicle for understanding yourself, as this inner awareness comes to you through inner pictures, words, thoughts, sensations, or feelings.

USING GUIDED IMAGERY

As you can see from reading the explanations above, visualization and guided imagery aren't synonymous. Although the majority of people do see pictures in their mind's eye, guided imagery is more than just visualization. Guided imagery draws on all the senses and creates a feeling in your mind and body. For the purposes of this book, I'll be using the words "guided imagery" as an all-inclusive term, encompassing vision, touch, hearing, smelling, and inner sensations.

Energizing your imagination with guided imagery lets you tap into your mind's power and turn your dreams into reality. It's actually fairly simple to call forth the mental pictures, sensory images, and the emotions of a good time. When you open your eyes, you may be surprised to notice how calm and peaceful you now feel.

The Ogre of Self-Doubt

I can't.

I'll never be able to.

I always say the wrong things.

I'll make a fool of myself.

I'll probably blow it.

You know, I've always wanted to _____, but I just don't know where to begin.

Do any of these statements sound familiar? If so, you're not alone! Self-doubt affects millions of men and women from all walks of life each and every day. Certainly from time to time each of us feels we're not the most self-assured person in the world, whether we're asking someone out on a date, giving a presentation at work, summoning the courage to ask the boss for a raise, or dealing with the anxiety that arises when we look at the latest ideal of physical perfection on a magazine cover. But when self-doubt begins to rule your life you become crippled, believing you're "less than," "just not good enough," or "never going to." When these thoughts and feelings take over your life, you watch your dreams and confidence slip farther and farther away.

Self-doubt is the insidious ogre in your mind that hijacks your feelings of achievement and happiness. It can be the constantly nagging voice inside your head or the worry that makes you toss and turn at four in the morning, the gremlin that gnaws away at your relationships or saps your energy at work. This ogre undermines your confidence, trips you up, drains your strength, and generally makes you feel horrible. Self-doubt can feel like an alien invasion, zapping you as if with a laser, stopping you cold in your tracks. Self-doubt keeps you stuck and immobilized.

Self-doubt keeps you from living the life you're meant to live. Those pesky and irritating voices of self-doubt prevent you from getting the guy or girl, meeting your quotas, or starting a new chapter in your career. Self-doubt ties you up in knots, makes you sick to your stomach, or makes you so scared you want to crawl into a hole and pull the covers over your head.

Yet, we all need to ask ourselves the following important questions about our self-doubt:

- Where does self-doubt come from?

- How does self-doubt have the power to do this to me?

- Why does self-doubt make me feel so helpless, hopeless, and defeated?

- How can I conquer the monstrous ogre in my mind that preys upon me morning, noon, and night?

Imagery can serve as a key that unlocks your positive dreams, which self-doubt and fear have held hostage in your mind. Let's see how.

Living Life Free from Self-Doubt

What if I told you that the tools of guided imagery can quiet the nagging self-doubt in your head and create self-confidence? What would you say if I told you that these simple tools will help you feel strong, sure of yourself, and full of vigor and happiness? What if I told you that using the power of guided imagery on a daily basis doesn't have any negative side effects and can be used without a prescription? What if I said that you don't need an extreme plastic-surgery makeover to feel better or simply feel good?

Would you like to learn more about this?

You might automatically respond by saying, "That's impossible. I've tried everything and this is just how I am. Imagination is a bunch of hocus-pocus and new-age false hope. And besides, it simply doesn't work."

Not so. Guided imagery has been empirically studied in hundreds of scientific investigations. These studies have shown it to be effective in addressing issues such as chronic pain, arthritis, fibromyalgia, post-traumatic stress disorder, headaches, and irritable bowel syndrome. If it can do all of these things, then guided imagery can certainly help you overcome your self-doubt. And, there is scientific proof that you can!

Martin Rossman, a physician and board-certified acupuncturist who has practiced holistic medicine since 1972, states in his book *Guided Imagery for Self-Healing*, "literally thousands of scientific studies have demonstrated the attitudinal, emotional, and behavioral effects" (2000, 7) using the natural healing abilities of our imagination. Research in eye movement desensitization and reprocessing (EMDR), biofeedback, hypnosis, prayer, yoga, meditation, and creative visualization has documented a remarkable capacity for humans to use visualization and guided imagery in a relaxed state of mind. Yet, as Dr. Rossman states, there is still resistance in the medical community and the general population to the idea that the body and the mind are connected. Let's take a few moments to consider what types of resistance may come up for you. Before beginning the exercise below, begin a fresh page in your notebook and title it "Ways in Which Self-Doubt Stops Me Cold."

Awareness Exercise #1

In what areas of your life do you feel the most self-doubt? You might be reading this book for any number of reasons, but chances are you picked it up because of the title. Take a few brief moments to think about your self-doubt and consider this basic question: in what ways does self-doubt stop you cold?

1. In your notebook, list three ways that self-doubt stops you cold, limits you, or stops you from getting what you want. You may have more than one area of your life where self-doubt keeps you from accomplishing your goals. Some examples are looking for a new job, starting an exercise plan, preparing to run a marathon, losing weight, improving your sex life, writing the great American novel or a Hollywood screenplay, having more friends, improving your personal relationships, beginning to date after a

divorce, or giving better presentations at work. Whatever comes to your mind, just jot down the first three things you think of. If you can't think of three, that's okay. If you come up with more than three, that's okay too.

2. After you've listed how self-doubt limits you, think about your beliefs associated with each of these areas. Beliefs could be something like the following:

   • I'm too old to get a new job.

   • I just don't have the motivation to stick to my exercise program.

   • Who'd want to date me after twenty-five years of marriage?

3. In your notebook, write down your beliefs about your self-doubt.

Congratulations! You've taken your first steps toward renewed self-confidence. However, having completed this exercise, you might be automatically saying, "See, I was right. Of course I'm too _____ [old, lazy, or undesirable, for example] to do what I want to do." Let's now take a quick look at where self-doubt comes from and begin to rid yourself of its insidious and false control.

Where Self-Doubt Comes From: The Inner Critic

As children we start out full of confidence in our abilities and strengths, with unlimited creative imaginations. Free from self-doubt, we are eager to try out new things and explore new worlds. It's only as we grow older that we start to evaluate our behavior, second-guess ourselves, and judge ourselves against others. And, as a result of hard knocks and disappointments, our self-confidence takes a beating.

Self-doubt comes first and foremost from our inner critic. (See the Resources section at the end of this book for a list of good books that address the voice of the inner critic.) Let's consider how the inner critic sabotages our confidence.

THE INFLUENCE OF OUR FAMILIES

When we're young, our parents or caregivers are ideally trying to keep us safe and warm, encouraging us to look both ways before we cross the street and to stay away from hot burners. Yet, their actions, reactions, and disapproval when we've misbehaved become distorted and lodged in our memories, our bodies, and our emotions. Over time, what was at first an external voice of caution becomes an internalized distortion of the truth. Hal and Sidra Stone (1993) describe the inner critic as whispering, whining, and needling us into place. It checks our thoughts, controls our behavior, and inhibits our actions. While the inner critic thinks it's keeping us safe and warm and protecting us from being disliked, hurt, or abandoned, it really acts as a negative inner voice that causes shame, anxiety, depression, and low self-esteem. The inner critic can be a powerful saboteur of our relationships and self-confidence.

THE INFLUENCE OF TRAUMATIC EVENTS

The inner critic not only comes from parents and caregivers in our early lives, but also from life situations and circumstances that leave us traumatized in some way. Were you ever ridiculed in grade school? Over the years these kinds of internalized traumas, memories, and mental images hold us back and stop us cold. The inner critic can pop up spontaneously. We become like Pavlov's dogs: the minute something happens that challenges our self-confidence, a little bell goes off in our mind and we automatically respond with old patterns of thinking and behaving. These distorted patterns are embedded in our consciousness, dictating our behavior without enabling us to decide whether this response is still appropriate. Self-doubt and the inner critic go hand in hand. But, while we can never totally get rid of it, we can learn to identify the inner critic's defeating voice. And, in doing so, we can transform the inner critic into an ally.

The inner critic not only shows up in the unwanted inner voice but also in imagery, where it can take any form. For example, the image of the inner critic could be a dark rain cloud hanging over our head, following us everywhere we go. The inner critic might appear to us as a hobgoblin, a pecking bird, a deceased relative, or a crazy witch. My own inner critic shows up as the Wicked Witch of the West, with her ominous "I'll get you, and your little dog too!"

What Does Your Inner Critic Look Like?

Let's spend some time finding an image of your inner critic.

Awareness Exercise #2

1. Allow yourself to sit in a comfortable chair, and let yourself relax.

2. Close your eyes and know that you are perfectly safe and focus on your breathing.

3. Begin to let the inner critic's voice communicate to you. What is the critic saying? What does it want you to pay attention to?

4. In your mind's eye, ask the inner critic its name.

5. Make sure you get a good sense of what the inner critic looks like before you say good-bye. Open your eyes.

6. Now, take up a pencil and pad, and sketch out a picture of your inner critic. Or, if you're not comfortable drawing, start browsing through magazines. As you flip through the pages of the magazines, be on the lookout for a photograph, an image, or partial image that resembles your inner critic. Cut out the picture. You might find that the picture you've drawn or cut out is the Wicked Witch of the West, a dark rain cloud, a wily fox, Godzilla, or an ogre— it doesn't matter what it is, as long as it makes sense to you.

    Perhaps you've come up with several images, photographs, or drawings. That's okay too. But if you haven't come across a photograph or image that represents your inner critic, I'd encourage you to keep looking and sketching. You may one day find yourself shouting "That's my inner critic!" while thumbing through magazines in a doctor's or dentist's waiting room.

THE MANY FACES OF YOUR INNER CRITIC

A visual representation of the inner critic may take several different forms for each of us, depending on the situations in which we find ourselves. For me, the Wicked Witch of the West, with her green skin and menacing, snarling, threatening voice, is a strong and emotionally charged image. Also, when I'm feeling backed into a corner, stuck or "frozen" in my tracks, the towering black monolith from the movie *2001: A Space Odyssey* hovers directly in front of my mind's eye (you'll understand why toward the end of this chapter).

Susan, a former student of mine, found her inner critic to be a proper Victorian woman. She came across a photograph in a magazine one day of a woman wearing a long black dress with a high button collar, a whalebone corset, and black lace-up shoes, sitting ramrod straight with her hair pulled back into a severe bun. For Susan this very stuffy and constricting image was full of disapproval and harsh judgment. John, a former coaching client, drew a stormy rain cloud hovering over his head as he walked down a sidewalk. In John's drawing, the rain cloud was dumping rain only on him, while the other people in his drawing were happily walking under clear, sunny skies.

Having given your inner critic a visual sense and a name, you now have a way of identifying it when it shows up in your life. This helps you to remember that the inner critic isn't you, but rather a representation of a protective inner mechanism that's run amok. Now you've accomplished the first step toward using imagery for self-confidence!

When I first asked my own inner critic what its name was, the Wicked Witch hissed at me, "You know my name!" and proceeded to chastise me further for not recognizing her very famous Hollywood face. Susan asked her inner critic this question, and in her imagination she "heard" the name Lady Constriction, indeed a very proper English Victorian woman. For John, Chief Rain Cloud announced its intention to always hover overhead, drenching his confidence in self-doubt.

WHEN THE INNER CRITIC IS MOM OR DAD

Did your drawing or image of your inner critic resemble either of your parents, or perhaps a relative or a former teacher? Instead of drawing a picture or looking through magazines, maybe you went directly to your family photo album. Actually, this isn't at all uncommon. As you learned earlier, the inner critic starts out as a warning system from principal caregivers and, as we grow older, transforms into the ever-present internal negative voice. Yet it's important to remember that this exercise isn't about placing blame on your parents, grandparents, or any authority figure from your past. This exercise is merely about bringing the critic into a visual awareness, in order to help you become alert to its power and eliminate its negative effects.

Using the Power of Your Imagination for Self-Confidence

Where would the world be if Michelangelo had said, "I can't paint the Sistine Chapel"? Imagine what might have happened if Christopher Columbus had said, "I couldn't possibly sail in that little boat." Or if the Wright brothers had said, "Fly like a bird? You're irrational!" Where would we be if early men and women hadn't smoothed out the sides of a boulder to make a wheel? Or if John F. Kennedy had said, "A man on the moon? That's impossible!"

Throughout the course of history, humans have made progress each and every step of the way because someone had a visual image of how things could be better or different. Michelangelo imagined the figures he carved emerging out of the stone. He felt that all he had to do was remove that which didn't belong there, and he visualized the finished sculpture revealing itself as he worked. Columbus imagined a new route to the Far East even while many scholars told him the world was flat. The Wright brothers imagined that man could fly in the air, and John F. Kennedy's vision of a man on the moon energized and motivated the best scientific minds to make it into a reality.

Olympic athletes use the power of guided imagery all the time. Surely you've heard interviews with Olympic athletes saying they imagined in their mind's eye the perfect balance beam routine, landing the triple axel, or swimming with power, grace, and speed. These athletes imagine themselves standing on the podium, hearing the crowd cheer and their national anthem played, and seeing their flag raised high while a medal is hung around their neck.

But you don't have to be an Olympic athlete to use the power of guided imagery to improve your life. Imagine, if you will, how much better your life would be if, instead of focusing on the negative thoughts and images in your mind, you rechanneled that time and energy toward focusing on your strengths: Focusing on what's right with you and all that you're capable of doing and achieving. Focusing the power of your mental pictures to realize yourself being strong, successful, and confident. Once you have clarified these visions of inspiration, you can indeed transform your dreams into reality.

Backed into a Corner and Unable to Get Out

When I was about five years old my parents bought a new upright freezer. The old freezer was left at the back of the house to be picked up when the new one was delivered. I remember that hot summer day very well. My next-door neighbor, Buddy, and I were playing Superman. There wasn't anything Superman couldn't do. In fact, Superman could run faster, jump higher, and even burst through solid doors! I wanted to be like Superman. Buddy and I took turns swinging on the door of the old freezer, getting inside, and, just before the door closed, bursting out and yelling "Superman!"

After we played for a while, Buddy got called home to lunch. But I didn't want to stop playing. I climbed into the freezer—in fact, into the lowest part of the freezer, below one of the shelves. The door slammed shut and locked. When I tried to burst open the door with my Superman yell, the door wouldn't budge. I was trapped inside.

The memories, visual images, and feelings are still crystal clear in my mind today. It was pitch black inside. And hot, very hot. The shelf pressed against my back, hard and unmoving. There wasn't any room to maneuver inside. I could feel the walls of the freezer closing in on me, pressing back against my legs and sides. I was crouched down inside on all fours. I screamed. I yelled. I cried. I lashed out, hitting the sides, top, and walls of the freezer with my fists. I vomited on myself and ultimately I passed out. I was backed into a corner and I couldn't get out no matter how hard I fought.

The next thing I remember is opening my eyes and looking up into the beautiful blue sky. Somehow I was outside the freezer and lying on the cool grass. My sisters, Patricia and Carolyn, had been looking after me that day. It was my lunchtime and they had gone all around the neighborhood looking for me, to no avail. As they walked back to the house, for some reason they decided to open the freezer door. I rolled out, unconscious and blue.

Now, the point of this story is not so much in the actual occurrence, but rather how, over the decades, it played a significant and often unconscious role in my life, affecting my beliefs and my behavior, and sapping my self-confidence in a number of ways. Gradually, with the help of several qualified professionals, I realized that whenever I was metaphorically or symbolically backed into a corner or felt there was no way out, I would come out swinging with all my might, and when that didn't work I would shut down emotionally. I didn't have the self-confidence to find my way out of uncomfortable situations. When I wanted to explore the world, the inner critic would say, "Don't—you'll get backed into a corner and you won't be able to get out." Along with this belief, the image of a stark black monolith always appeared before me: unyielding, ominous, and literally taking my breath away. Consequently, for many years and in several areas of my life, I stayed "stuck." I didn't know how to explore new and interesting situations, such as when I'd outgrown a job or a relationship. And if I did find myself getting backed into a corner, metaphorically or symbolically, I would lose my self-confidence and my belief that I could manage my way to safety or freedom.

Working with trained professionals, I used a variety of guided imagery techniques to reduce the power this experience held over me. Over the course of this book, you'll learn about these very same techniques, and read about the process I used to free myself from the self-doubt that kept me from exploring new opportunities or getting out of a tight squeeze. Now, certainly this is an extreme illustration of the dramatic impact life situations, events, and inner dialogue can have. I offer it here because it demonstrates two key points:

1. Events, situations, memories, and mental pictures become lodged in our minds, affecting our behavior and keeping us uncomfortably stuck.

2. Self-defeating behavior can be addressed by using guided imagery.

The Big Picture

What a great start you've made in this chapter. You have made a good assessment of your confidence level, you've identified how self-doubt stops you from pursuing goals, you've identified your inner critic with an image and a name, and you've experienced the initial steps toward using guided imagery for relaxation. Let's now move forward and identify how your attitudes, beliefs, behavior, and thoughts affect your self-image, and learn how to use guided imagery to visualize confidence.

2

the fundamentals of guided imagery

"Imagination is everything. It is the preview of life's coming attractions." —Albert Einstein

Imagery forms in the mind long before you acquire the ability to use verbal language, allowing you to store memories, plan for future possibilities, creatively fantasize, and move from anxiety to courage. You use imagery instinctively all day long, whenever you daydream or project your wants and desires into the future (Bresler and Rossman 2004).

Imagery Is a Natural Language

If someone were to ask you to describe your living room, you would re-create (in your mind) the experience of being in your living room. In answering you'd make use of imagery to retrieve the information. For example, if I were to re-create in my mind the experience of being in my own living room, I'd say, "Well, it has red drapes, a sage-colored love seat, a nice warm fire in the fireplace, scented candles, soft music playing, the dog curled up on my lap, and morning sunlight streaming in through the windows." When recalling this room, I've used visual, kinesthetic, smell, and feeling senses to "see" this room in my mind and to convey it to you. Clearly, the imagery is more than just tangibles, but rather the whole feeling of being in this room.

The Mind-Body Bridge

Your mind and body communicate using imagery like a bridge. The bridge between the mind and body happens all the time and is as effortless as breathing. Let's take a short look at how this mind-body bridge works and how it influences the pictures that form in our minds.

HOW GUIDED IMAGERY WORKS

The brain, the most complex organ in the human body, determines how we function. As such, it plays a significant role in how guided imagery works.

In the late 1950s and early 1960s, significant research was conducted by Roger Sperry, a neuropsychologist at the California Institute of Technology. Sperry's work later earned him a Nobel Prize in Medicine for identifying two separate functions of the brain. Sperry's work identified that each part of the brain specializes in its own style of thinking and has different capabilities (Sperry, Zaidel, and Zaidel 1979). Sperry and his colleagues were attempting to find a solution or treatment for people with epileptic seizures. Patients who had been diagnosed with epilepsy consented to surgery to have the corpus callosum, the nerve bundle that transmits signals between the left and right hemispheres of the brain, surgically cut in an effort to control their seizures. During his research process, Sperry made an amazing discovery: he found that each half of the brain had its own conscious thought process and its own memories and that the left and right hemispheres of the brain had specializations. Although Sperry's research was often trivialized or misrepresented in the media (which sometimes reported, incorrectly, that the two brain hemispheres are largely unconnected), his findings help us understand how guided imagery works.

Sperry generalized that the left hemisphere of the brain specializes in rational and linear and critical thinking of the conscious mind. This left hemisphere is great for figuring out puzzles, balancing your checkbook, and even doing your taxes. It's an enormously necessary part of the brain and, as health psychologist David Bresler told me, "It's what makes us most human" (D. Bresler, pers. comm.).

The right hemisphere of the brain, however, is the seat of language, creativity, and emotions. This hemisphere specializes in the unconscious mind, the inner world of fantasy and insight. This part of the brain thinks holistically and intuitively, can see the big picture, and is spatially oriented and imaginatively charged. The right hemisphere of your brain is focused on relationships of patterns and can put things together in fresh, creative ways.

Guided imagery specifically utilizes the right hemisphere of the brain. You may have naturally experienced the power of your right hemisphere when you've struggled with thinking up a solution to a vexing problem that has kept you tossing and turning all night long. However, when you wake up in the morning with a sudden insight or solution, it's the right hemisphere of your brain that has been at work finding that solution.

The Science Behind the Power of Belief

When we are stressed, adrenaline and other chemicals and hormones rush through our bodies. The sight of a snake induces physical changes that prepare us to fight or flee, for example. These reactions occur in the face of both real and perceived threats. The brain doesn't know the difference between your boss pressuring you for a report and your perceived pressure to avoid losing your job. We know from clear scientific studies that our beliefs therefore affect our brains.

In a landmark 2005 study, associate professor of psychiatry and radiology Jon-Kar Zubieta and his colleagues at the University of Michigan documented that the power of belief actually activates systems in the brain that are directly related to experience. Zubieta injected a stinging concentrated saltwater solution into the jaw muscles of fourteen healthy young men to create temporary pain. Following these injections, these young men underwent a positron-emission tomography (PET) scan to detect changes in the brains based on the power of beliefs. During one scan, the young men were told that they would be getting a placebo, or fake injection, when in fact they were getting more salt water. The researchers told these men that the injection was going to help them tolerate pain. Despite the fact that the additional saltwater injection had no intrinsic therapeutic value, the researchers were amazed to find that the mere belief of pain relief translated into a physical reality. The simple belief that they were getting a drug to alleviate their pain caused chemical messengers in the brains of these fourteen young men to release the brain's natural painkillers, endorphins. This wasn't a trick or a sham. It wasn't magic. Instead, it was a natural and normal reaction to their belief that they were experiencing pain relief. The release of the endorphins was directly related to how much the young men believed the drug was going to be effective! Can you imagine how belief in yourself can trigger your own endorphins for confidence?

THE CHEMISTRY OF THE BRAIN AND IMAGERY

We're all born with billions of brain cells called neurons. Although these neurons are interrelated to each other, they don't actually touch. Between each of the neurons is a small gap, or synapse, which can be imagined as similar to a spark plug. As you think about giving a presentation at work or even going on a trip to Italy, chemicals, or neurotransmitters, jump between the synapses. These chemicals jumping from one nerve ending to another put on a glorious fireworks display and travel from your brain to the tips of your toes.

As these chemicals travel around your body all sorts of reactions begin to happen. If you're imagining the presentation at work, these chemicals are what cause you to feel anxiety. If you're imagining a relaxing trip to Italy, these same chemicals are responsible for the smile that appears on your face and the feeling of joy and anticipation associated with your vacation image. Because the brain can't tell the difference between an imagined or a real event, the mere belief of a positive or negative event causes associated neurotransmitters to surge throughout your body. The different feelings are in fact caused by the different chemicals.

Using Guided Imagery Actively and Consciously

The key to using guided imagery to develop healthy self-confidence begins with an active purpose. For example, it's not effective to simply let random pictures roam around in your head as you would in a daydream. A daydream, while enjoyable, doesn't involve focusing with a purpose.

To focus with an active purpose means that you're deliberately reinforcing thoughts and imagery that are conducive to self-confidence. When you actively engage in imagining what you want to be true, and focus your mind on creating positive conditions for your future success, your mind accepts this as truth and begins to act accordingly.

Effective leaders actively and purposefully use guided imagery when they convey their vision of success to their employees or team members. A good leader will motivate by describing his or her vision in full sensory detail, calling forth the feelings of winning in every member of the team. The group of people becomes unified, directed, and on target. In other words, they now have an active purpose.

Next time you are in a meeting with your boss or the CEO of your company, tune in to whether these leaders use a mental picture to convey their vision. In doing so, they'll be speaking to everyone's attitudes, beliefs, behaviors, and thought processes.

1. Take a moment and list in your journal three times in your life when you were confident.

2. Take another moment and list in your journal three times in your life when you weren't so confident.

Tools for Guided Imagery Success

I'm sure you have several questions about what guided imagery is, how to use it, and how it works. Now, let's look at the fundamentals of guided imagery.

TYPES OF GUIDED IMAGERY

There are several different types of imagery that are used for general health and well-being that you can use for developing confidence. Let's take a look at each one of them and discover how they work.

Directive Imagery

Directive imagery is imagery that is deliberately constructed; in other words, you consciously choose and construct the focus of your attention. For example, you can direct your mind to see active images of speaking in public, telling yourself to imagine the size of the auditorium, see the audience, hear the music that precedes your presentation, and imagine walking up to the podium. You can also use directive imagery to identify the tension in your body when you're asking someone out for a date, or telling someone a difficult truth; you may notice that your throat tightens up or your back muscles suddenly seem tied up in knots, for example. When you use directive imagery you deliberately see the muscles in your back smoothing out, the bands of tension relaxing, your shoulders dropping, your mouth softening, and your throat opening up so you can speak assuredly. Directive imagery is often used for recovery from illness or surgery. For example, some people have used directive imagery to see their bodies' white blood cells as white knights in shining armor doing battle with cancer cells.

Receptive Imagery

Using receptive imagery, also called insight imagery, you allow images to spontaneously "bubble up" into your mind from your deep unconscious, allowing the mind and body to listen to what is being said. When using this type of imagery you don't deliberately create the images as you do in directive imagery; rather, you see what pops into your head. Often these images are full of symbolic meaning; they can be of a religious figure, a guardian angel, or some other thing that might not immediately make sense to you. For example, you might be using guided imagery to practice standing up for yourself; yet the image that naturally pops into your mind is one of a jellyfish. With some reflection you might remember the first time you tried to stand up for yourself and someone told you that you were spineless. The image of the jellyfish provides an opportunity for tremendous insight: you may now see that your confidence level is connected with your belief that you don't have the backbone to stand up for yourself. Other examples of receptive imagery that could come up as images of self-doubt might be a dog nipping at your heels or a black crow pecking at your front door. Sharon, who felt an overwhelming sense of self-doubt, saw herself as wallpaper being painted over. After some reflection she was able to understand that she connected wallpaper with the idea of a wallflower, or a person who's always fading into the background.

Process or Step-by-Step Imagery

Process imagery, also called imagery rehearsal, helps you imagine each and every step you will take, in a proper sequence, to reach your final confidence goal. With process guided imagery you imagine in great detail how you want to accomplish your goal. Athletes use process imagery frequently. For instance, if you're using guided imagery to increase your confidence skills as a competitor in tennis, you would imagine the perfect swing of your racket and the movement of the tennis ball coming at you, and then you would picture in vivid detail each and every move your body makes as you return the shot. Process imagery is nearly always used in association with end-state imagery, which we'll talk about next.

End-State Imagery

End-state imagery involves seeing yourself accomplishing the goal you've set out to reach. You see yourself winning the tennis game. Or you imagine yourself getting the job, getting the guy or girl, walking down the aisle, receiving a larger paycheck after asking for a raise, or having good times with new friends. End-state imagery is enormously pleasant to experience because playing in your mind is a movie of exactly how you want it to be. But it's important to know that end-state imagery works best when it's utilized with step-by-step imagery. Both of these techniques reinforce each other and anchor the way you want to be into your mind and body.

Evocative Imagery

Evocative imagery is used to develop awareness of a specific quality, mood, or attitude that may be useful to you at any given time. This type of imagery works well in situations when you would like to have more of a given quality, such as confidence. Whenever you feel like you don't have enough of what you need, you can use evocative imagery to call it forth. For example, to use evocative imagery, recall a time in the past when you experienced having the quality of confidence. Imagine you are there right now. Notice how it feels to be back in this confident time and use your imagination to amplify this feeling. You can imagine you have a remote control and can turn up the volume as you would on a television or radio. You have the ability to control exactly how much you increase the volume, until you notice the feeling of confidence growing stronger and stronger. Next, with this feeling firmly planted in your mind, imagine using your remote control to fast-forward to the time and place in the future where you want more confidence. In your imagination, you can obtain the quality of confidence by simply using your imaginary remote control.

GUIDED IMAGERY AND RELAXATION

Guided imagery goes hand in hand with relaxation. Relaxation is a key to activating your creative imagination. When you're relaxed, your mind is more receptive to new imagery. Relaxation in itself enhances your health, performance, and self-esteem, and boosts your confidence. Guided imagery exercise 1 in the introduction begins with directions for relaxation to help calm your mind and body, creating a fertile ground for new imagery to take root.

Each time you use guided imagery, plan to spend at least twenty to thirty minutes to get the full benefit from the relaxation and the exercises. Most people find it best to set aside time in the morning and before going to sleep each night. As you become accustomed to the process, you can use guided imagery whenever you find yourself most in need. Remember each time to fully embrace the images that come to your mind. Don't dismiss them as silly or useless.

Ultimately, guided imagery will become part of your everyday routine. You'll find yourself unwinding, lightening up, letting go, slowing down, chilling out, and becoming more attuned to colors, textures, sounds, and smells in vibrant new ways. Calm and more serene, you'll also start to increase your creativity, as you move toward resolving inner conflicts, managing anxiety, and becoming more confident.

YOU ARE ALWAYS IN CONTROL

Guided imagery isn't about losing or giving up control of your mind. There are no hidden messages in the guided imagery exercises in this book. No one will control your thoughts. There will be no dangling pocket watches to make you cluck like a chicken! Guided imagery is just like getting lost in any activity that is pleasing to you, such as watching a movie, gardening, or reading a good book. Guided imagery is a tool everyone can use. And with repeated practice you will become more confident each day.

WHAT IF YOU GET BAD IMAGES?

This is a very common question. Images and visual representations in and of themselves aren't bad. However, the meaning that we attach to an image is highly personal, and we can interpret an image as positive or negative. If you should have an upsetting image come up, remember that you're in control at all times. The image comes from within you and is accompanied by an enormous amount of information and may be conveying something important. Look beyond the obvious and tune in to the message. Simply put, it's a vehicle to help you understand what is underneath your awareness.

WHAT IF YOU GET NO IMAGES?

This too is a very common question. As mentioned previously, not everyone "sees" these pictures in their heads, as if they were watching a movie. If you don't see pictures in your mind, don't worry. Instead, shift your attention to your other senses. What do you feel? What do you intuitively sense? What do you smell, hear, or taste? Use all of your senses to fully experience in your imagination the step-by-step process that will ultimately take you to your desired goal of overcoming self-doubt and living confidently.

CAN YOU USE AFFIRMATIONS WITH YOUR GUIDED IMAGERY?

Absolutely! Affirmations are extremely positive tools. Paired with guided imagery, affirmations are even more influential. Form an image for your affirmations. Reaffirm a new self-image for yourself each and every day. You can write your affirmations on an index card or sticky note and place them on your bathroom mirror, car dashboard, or computer monitor as daily reminders.

But be aware that affirmations alone may not overcome all your self-doubt. Affirmations used in association with guided imagery become more powerful and create self-confidence. Write your affirmations in the present tense and focus on what you want rather than on what you don't want.

One the following page are some examples of effective affirmations that you can use with your guided imagery:

- I expect the best and recognize when it comes to me.

- I communicate my feelings and thoughts with confidence.

- My confidence is growing daily.

- I always succeed!

- I *am* successful!

- I'm confident because I'm guided by my higher power.

- I now let go of all tension and stress, and I'm relaxed.

- I'm at ease with all those I meet.

- I'm full of peace and sure of myself.

- I now see my life as a wondrous, miraculous journey.

THE BENEFITS OF GUIDED IMAGERY

Guided imagery is a powerful and effective use of the creative imagination. As the communication bridge between the body and mind, the benefits of guided imagery are substantial—they can affect our attitudes, change our beliefs, and motivate new behavior. Guided imagery has been an important tool for healing and self-confidence in a number of societies around the world, including the health systems of Ayurvedic, Chinese, Japanese, European, Hindu, Tibetan, ancient Greek, Egyptian, and Native American cultures (Achterberg, Dossey, and Kolkmeier 1994; Rossman 2000, 2003). Guided imagery can do all of the following:

- Relieve stress, anxiety, depression, and physical and psychological symptoms

- Reduce pain and distress

- Help you stop smoking

- Motivate you to lose weight

- Focus your mind for peak performance

- Stimulate your body's immune response

- Reduce feelings of helplessness and hopelessness

- Treat you as a whole person and enhance your sense of overall well-being

- Increase self-management and coping skills

- Reduce nausea from chemotherapy and lower the need for postoperative medication

- Melt away your fears

- Resolve inner conflicts

- Develop your self-confidence

Using Guided Imagery to Find a Personal Place

Let's now practice a guided imagery script. Take time to work with this script before moving on to the remainder of the book. Become very familiar with the opening steps of this exercise because you'll return to them time and time again in your daily practice. It is a good way to enter into a state of deep relaxation, which is conducive to developing strong self-confidence.

We all have times when we know we're "in the flow" of life. We're prepared, we're sure of our skills and talents, we feel on top of the world, and things come easily. Before starting, go back and review the responses that you jotted down in awareness exercise 3. Select one of the three times when you felt very confident. You'll focus on that experience in this exercise.

Guided Imagery Exercise #2

1. *Take the phone off the hook and do whatever you can to create a quiet space for the next twenty minutes. Sit in a comfortable chair, with your feet flat on the floor, and allow yourself to relax. Kick off your shoes and loosen any tight clothing or belts.*

2. *Close your eyes and know that you are perfectly safe. Begin to take some slow, deep breaths.*

   Breathe slowly and deeply, your belly rising and falling. Inhale . . . and exhale. Inhale . . . and exhale. Inhale . . . and exhale. Let the stress of the day melt away. When you sense an inner calmness and relaxation, you'll find that your body is relaxing with each breath. You are safe, protected, and alert.

3. *While paying attention to your breathing, now begin to imagine a ball of clear light hanging directly over your head, bathing you in a warm glow. This light feels good. This light feels warm, and you know that with each ray caressing your body you're protected and nourished.*

4. *As you feel this clear, clean, warm light slowly flowing over your body, you begin to notice your scalp and forehead relax. Your face relaxes, your neck and shoulders relax, your chest feels warm, and your deep breathing gets deeper and deeper.*

5. *As the warm, protective light flows down your chest and into your belly, it too begins to relax. The light continues down your hips, your thighs, and your legs. Finally, as it relaxes your feet, the warm light drains out of the bottom of your feet all the way down deep into the earth. You're now deeply relaxed, safe, and secure.*

6. *As you enjoy this good feeling, begin to imagine that you are in a beautiful place outdoors. This can be any place, perhaps a spot that you've visited or a place only in your imagination. This is your special personal place where magical things can and will happen.*

7. *Spend a few moments enjoying your personal place. Find a comfortable place to sit or stretch out. You may find an old hollow log or a rock to sit upon. You realize that your body perfectly fits, as if it were made just for you.*

8. *As you sit or stretch out, enjoy how good it feels to be here. What time of day is it? What are you wearing? What is the weather like? Do you hear sounds? Are there any aromas? Allow yourself to be in this moment in time and feel it with as much intensity as you choose. Simply allow yourself to spend as much time in your special place as you choose.*

9. *When you are ready, you can allow the images to fade. You can say good-bye to your personal place for now and slowly begin to come back to the present time and place. Take a few energizing breaths, wiggle your toes and fingers, and begin to stretch your body.*

10. *When you're ready, slowly open your eyes, feeling refreshed, happy, and calm. Fully awake, tell yourself that you can return to this place whenever you want by simply imagining it in your mind's eye and noticing how good it feels. Record your special place in your notebook as before.*

11. *When you have some time, flip through magazines and look for images that represent your personal, beautiful, special place. You can also sketch a drawing or pull a photograph from your family photo album if it's a place that you have been to before. Paste these images or drawings in your confidence notebook and jot down some notes or write about your experience.*

The Big Picture

In this chapter you've learned that imagery is a natural language used by all people all the time. Images are neither bad nor good. When you interpret your images using words, the meaning you attach is a reflection of your experience and a bridge connecting your body and mind. You've learned that guided imagery is done actively and with purpose; you've listed times in your life when you were confident and times you weren't. You've learned that affirmations are useful in supporting your guided imagery as long as they are positive, are rooted in the present tense, and reinforce your confident self-image. Let's now move forward to understand how your beliefs, attitudes, behavior, and thoughts affect your self-confidence.

_3_

reclaiming your confidence

**"Follow your gut. Have confidence. We made it up as we
went along." —George Harrison**

There's an old belief that "perception is reality." What this means
is that whatever beliefs you hold determine your reality. Your
beliefs, then, are the glasses through which you see life. Beliefs are
very important, since they determine so much about your life.

It All Starts with a Belief

Whether you consciously realize it or not, you carry around in your
mind blueprints and images of the person you think you are. These

blueprints, which form your core beliefs, are very persuasive. If you believe yourself to be full of self-doubt, you will be.

How you describe yourself, using these blueprints, creates your self-image, or your general perception of your abilities, talents, and character. Who you believe you are and how you describe yourself say volumes about your attitudes, behavior, and motivation.

Your self-image is complete in every detail and governs how you act, regardless of whether or not it reflects reality. In fact, you'll always act in a way that is consistent with your core beliefs. It's human nature not to question the authority of your beliefs or resulting self-image—until it starts to impair your life. Because it is not questioned or challenged, your self-image is a distorted view built up over time, formed from past experiences, successes, and failures. Unfortunately, over the years your beliefs and self-image become so ingrained that you take them as the absolute truth: "That's just how I am."

Your beliefs and self-image lie at the core of who you think you are, and as a result they largely dictate the course of your life. Below are some of the ways that your beliefs and self-image influence your life:

- They determine what you know about the world.

- They distinguish how you make sense of life.

- They establish what you feel you deserve.

- They define your attitudes, behavior, and motivation.

- They determine your self-esteem.

- They create your future.

SELF-ESTEEM AND SELF-EFFICACY

High self-esteem is your belief that you are a good, worthy, and valuable person. An integral part of your self-image, it is essential to your overall health and well-being. Self-esteem can also be negative, just like self-imagery, and have a dramatic impact on your confidence. The ability to create an identity that allows you to have positive feelings about yourself is what distinguishes human beings from other animals. With either high or low self-esteem you evaluate and judge yourself as either good or bad. Matthew McKay and Patrick Fanning, in their book *Self-Esteem: A Proven Program of Cognitive Techniques for Assessing, Improving, and Maintaining Your Self-Esteem*, state that "this judging and rejecting yourself causes enormous pain. . . . You take fewer social, academic, and career risks" (2000, 1) when your self-esteem is compromised.

"Self-efficacy" is a term coined by social psychologist Albert Bandura. Self-efficacy, different from self-esteem, is the belief that you have the capabilities and skills necessary to complete what you set out to do. While the two are directly related to one another, there is an important distinction between self-esteem and self-efficacy. Self-esteem is about your sense of worth and value, whereas self-efficacy is about the perception you can reach your goal. For example, let's say you have healthy self-esteem and you know that you are smart. However, when it comes to downhill skiing, you continually fall down the slopes. You have healthy self-esteem, yet your self-efficacy may take a blow because you don't know how to ski.

So, if you see yourself as smart and capable, then you'll create confidence. Having a clear understanding of your personal value, your abilities, and your beliefs contributes to your confidence.

HOW DO YOU SEE YOURSELF?

Much like the inner critic, the power of your self-image, beliefs, self-esteem, and self-efficacy begins in early childhood. Parents, teachers, friends, culture, and even the school-yard bully all contribute to your beliefs.

How would you describe yourself? Do you see yourself as a good girl, a proper young lady, a bad boy, or a troublemaker? Are you competent, physically attractive, and friendly? Or are you moody, uncoordinated, and klutzy? Are you a geek? An airhead?

How do you describe your future? When you imagine yourself many years from now, do you see yourself as a loser, someone who just didn't make it, or do you envision the calm, confident person you've always dreamed of becoming? How you see yourself, your self-image snapshot, is about to get a makeover—changing from a picture of self-doubt to one of confidence.

Awareness Exercise #4

In your notebook, copy the sentence fragments below and then fill in the blanks to complete the sentences. Don't think about each statement too much. Whatever pops into your mind first is the best answer. This sentence completion exercise will help you uncover beliefs that may have been guiding your life up to now, and it will provide you with insight into the beliefs you have about your future.

As a young child, my favorite game was _____.

I remember I liked to _____.

I was praised in school for _____ .

My parents seemed to feel that I was _____ .

My own feeling was that I was _____ .

In my family I was considered _____ .

As a teenager, I felt _____ .

As a teenager, what made me feel confident was _____ .

The teacher who wrecked my confidence was _____ .

I believed this teacher because _____ .

My nickname or what the other kids called me was _____ .

The general message of my grade-school report cards
was _____ .

In my twenties I generally feel (will feel, or felt) _____ .

In my thirties I feel (will feel, or felt) that my life was ____ .

In my forties I believe (will believe, or believed) that ____ .

I yearn (will yearn, or yearned) to just _____ .

In my forties I tell (will tell, or told) myself _____ .

In my fifties I will make peace with (made peace with) __ .

My view of life is (will be, or was) _____ .

At sixty I have (will have) _____ *(handwritten: feelings, behavior, thinking, thoughts — triangle diagram)*

In my sixties I regret (think I will regret, or regretted) ____.

In my seventies I look forward (looked forward) to _____.

I choose to _____.

I will _____.

I can _____.

My focus _____.

My passion _____.

My joy _____.

As I turn (turned) eighty and move (moved) into my nineties I will (did) _____.

My concern about _____.

My acceptance of _____.

My self-image will be _____.

I want _____.

On my one hundredth birthday, I will _____.

I believe _____.

The ABCs of Self-Confidence

Self-confidence affords you the belief that, within reason, you do have the ability and skills to accomplish what you envision for yourself. Since confidence isn't with each of us all the time and in all situations, our beliefs and behavior can change according to the tasks and situations at hand. You can be confident in one area of your life but not in another. For example, you may be confident in math but not in biology. You may be confident in your academic abilities but not in sports. You may relish the excitement of giving a talk before a large crowd but feel awkward going on a first date.

Since self-confidence exists within the context of your own beliefs, self-image, self-esteem, self-efficacy, memories, and perceptions, it can be summed up in three terms: attitudes (how you feel), behavior (what you do), and cognitions (what you think).

ATTITUDES

Attitude is a key psychological concept. Made up of your moods and emotions, your attitude is the sum of the convictions you hold. Attitudes can be either negative or positive views of a person, event, or situation.

Has anyone ever said to you, or have you ever said to someone else, "You really have a bad attitude"? Having a bad attitude colors your beliefs, your images of yourself, and most certainly your behavior. Or, have you ever heard someone say about a person who has experienced very difficult or tragic events, "Can you believe what a good attitude she has, after all she's been through?" In the face of devastating news, some people seem to be able to move on and in some cases actually become better people. I recall one person with a terminal diagnosis telling me some years ago, "This diagnosis was the best thing that ever happened to me." How could this be? I asked. The person's response was "It's given me a clarity of purpose, put things into perspective, and now I'm not afraid of living life to the fullest anymore."

Wouldn't it be great if we could all have a strong sense of belief and conviction, without needing a diagnosis to give us a kick in the pants? It's these feeling-based attitudes that lead to the B in the ABCs of self-confident behavior.

BEHAVIOR

Your behavior is the actions or reactions you have in response to a person, event, or situation. Always in relationship to your environment, behavior can be conscious or unconscious, voluntary or involuntary. However, attitudes don't always predict behavior. You might believe that exercising is good for you, but you just can't seem to motivate yourself to change your behavior and go jogging.

Behavior is related to your nervous system, and humans, with our complex nervous systems, have a great capacity to learn new responses and adjust our behavior. Your behavior follows your attitudes and beliefs and can change in the direction of your beliefs.

Twelve-step programs for addiction recovery sometimes encourage "faking it till you make it" or "acting as if" in order to practice new behavior. This means that you can act as if you have the confidence you desire, and, with daily practice, you'll start to behave accordingly. Imagining yourself fully in command will put the B into your ABCs.

COGNITION

Cognition involves your memory, perceptions, judgments, and generally how you think about life and yourself. Specifically, we utilize the stories and pictures in our heads, called *schemas* by psychologists. Schemas, which make exceptional use of beliefs and images, are mental representations of concepts that we use in an unconscious process to help us know how to respond to new situations. When we encounter or anticipate new and unappealing situations, such as a dreaded sales meeting, or even meeting new people, the mind searches for memories of similar situations with which to compare the new or unknown ones. Cognition, or what you think about, links up with your attitudes and behavior like a triangle to form the basis of how you are in the world as a human being.

Together, your attitudes, behavior, and cognition form the ABCs of your confidence.

Awareness Exercise #5

1. In your notebook, write down twenty-five words, adjectives, beliefs, metaphors, or phrases that you think describe you. Write a short explanation of each and what it means to you. Ask five people for five words, adjectives, metaphors, or phrases that they think describe you. You can ask your friends, family, people you work with, people you've known for a long time, or even people that you've just met.

2. As you analyze these words and phrases, do you see any that appear more than once? How do you feel about the words and phrases? Are there any surprises? Are there any

disappointments? Do some people view you in very specific ways that you feel aren't really you anymore? Do any of the metaphors particularly ring a bell for you?

THE ABCs IN ACTION

Imagine that you've been told you have to make a public presentation before the entire marketing department at your office, or the local school board. Immediately, you think of this task as a dangerous experience. Why? Because, as mentioned above, your mind begins to rewind the tape in your head, looking for past self-image memories, experiences, and feelings that match "public speaking." Once a self-image memory is identified, the mind then projects it onto your mental movie screen and replays your experience of standing before your sixth-grade class giving a book report, for example.

Now, you may have had a good experience of giving a book report. If so, your schema will match up. "It was a good experience, and not as bad as I thought it was going to be. The teacher gave me an A, the other kids applauded, and Mom and Dad were very proud," you recall. "No sweat," you say. "This will be a piece of cake!"

However, if you had a bad experience of giving a book report, a negative schema kicks in. "What a horrible experience. I was mortified! My hands were clammy, I stuttered, I ran out of the room crying, and the teacher gave me a D." And then, to make matters worse, your inner critic steps up to remind you, "You can't speak in public! You've never been able to speak in public, and furthermore you'll never be able to!"

What's happened in the second scenario is that your schemas have retrieved all your beliefs and self-images to quickly come up with a response of self-doubt. "If I was unsuccessful in the past, then I'll be unsuccessful now." The evidence that you've recalled is telling you that because your previous experience was negative, the new experience will end up the same way. But you're no longer ten years old and there isn't a teacher in sight. The evidence, which seems to indicate that all public speaking is dangerous, is actually false, although it appears to be real. Your attitudes, behavior, and cognitive thoughts have all come together here to form the ABCs of self-confidence.

When your fearful schema of speaking in public joins forces with the inner critic, you forget that you're prepared. You forget that your facts and figures are accurate, your colleagues are supportive, you're an adult, and you don't have to drop everything and run.

THE GIFT OF GUIDED IMAGERY

This is where guided imagery tools are extremely effective and positive. Guided imagery has the ability to lessen your fears and change your attitudes, behavior, and cognitive thought process. Guided imagery empowers you to stand tall and confident. When you use guided imagery tools you are connecting your ABCs with tangible results. When you link your inspiration and courage of conviction, the result is "Yes, I believe in myself and I can make a difference in my life." You can then bring these well-defined and successful images into the reality of your life.

SELF-DEFEATING BELIEFS

When we subscribe to self-defeating beliefs that sap our confidence, we tend to do the following:

Think in black-and-white terms. Our belief and thinking is all or nothing. We might think, for example, "I failed the test, so from now on I'll fail all tests." Thinking in black and white causes us to see only the dark cloud hanging over our heads, like John did with Chief Rain Cloud, or feel limitations, like Susan did every time Lady Constriction showed up.

Magnify the critical, negative, and the unforgiving. When we have a bad attitude that magnifies the negative, we believe things like "I'm always a misfit," and "I'm always a loser."

Dismiss the positive and encouraging. We find ourselves unable to take in compliments or receive support from others.

Focus on what we didn't do. We might think, "If only I had _____, then I could have _____," or "I should have _____; then I would have _____."

Live in the past. You might find yourself saying, "If only things could be like they were before," "If only I were twenty-five again," or "If only I hadn't eaten that second piece of cake."

SOLUTIONS TO SELF-DEFEATING BELIEFS

When you find yourself encountering self-defeating beliefs, you can create solutions by trying some of the following ideas:

- Ask yourself, "Is there something else I'm not aware of?"

- Tell yourself, "Even though it happened like this in the past, that doesn't mean the same will happen in the future."

- Wonder out loud, "How might I be mistaken?"

- Ask "What else do I need to know, or what else might be important to know?"

- Determine whose voice you hear in your mind. Is it the inner critic? Is it your parent or child? What might an image of this voice look like?

- Cancel the old by imagining a red stop sign and replacing it with a new image, such as a gold medal or something else that reminds you of your strength.

- Use your affirmations.

- Imagine the old self-image fading like an old photograph.

Reclaiming Your Imagination

Now that you've identified some self-defeating beliefs, let's identify how you can use your creative imagination to move toward your self-confidence goals. As you've learned, we live in a culture that doesn't always value the power of creative imagination and innate creativity. We tend to think that the resources of the creative imagination are only for artists and craftsmen. We assume that guided imagery is not real and is nothing more than fantasy mumbo jumbo. You yourself may have likened your internal imagery to dreams, fantasies, and fairy tales. You might now be asking, "How did my inner imagery and imagination get such a bad rap?" It all started in what is now called the Age of Enlightenment.

THE AGE OF ENLIGHTENMENT

Ever since the beginning of the Age of Enlightenment in the seventeenth century, there's been a divide in Western culture between the body and the mind, science and spirituality, things that can be seen and things that can't be seen. René Descartes (1596–1650), unquestionably one of the most brilliant men who ever lived, was a seventeenth-century philosopher, mathematician, and scientist. For better or worse, Descartes' philosophical writings led to a shift in the way the mind and body were perceived. He viewed the mind (and the imagination) as separate from the body. Imagination, intuition, and spirituality became seen as separate and distinct functions not connected to the cognitive, rational, analytical, and objective mind. But, today, we're rediscovering the vital link between our imagination and our body, and we're learning how the mind-body connection works.

Your Personal Board of Directors

In order to reclaim your inner imagination, let's use the next awareness exercise to stretch your mental muscles and meet your supporters. Many for-profit and nonprofit organizations have groups of people who advise the management and staff regarding decisions, new products, and new directions. These advisers, sometimes called shareholders or trustees, are entrusted with the future of the company. Likewise, your personal board of directors is entrusted with your future as well. In your notebook, begin a new page and title it "My Board of Directors."

Awareness Exercise #6

1. Imagine you're planning a dinner party. You're creating the invitation list and you want to invite all the people who have inspired you over the years. These people can be real or imaginary, such as characters in a book or movie. They can be celebrities, inspirational philosophers, artists, scientists, religious figures, and even family members and friends. In your notebook list all the people or characters you'd like to invite to your dinner party.

2. Beside each name, write a few words or phrases explaining why this person is being invited. What is it about them that inspires you? How do they demonstrate confidence or creative imagination?

3. Next, try to find photographs or images of these people and paste them into your notebook.

4. Ask yourself, "How am I like this person or character?" Write your response in your notebook next to each person's photograph or image.

5. Last, if you find that question 4 doesn't bring anything to your immediate awareness, ask yourself, "How can I bring the inspirational and confident qualities of this person into my own life?"

NATURAL AND EASYGOING

Sammy was a thirty-five-year-old single man wanting to get married. He was shy and didn't feel confident about asking a woman for a date. He believed that he wasn't attractive or socially secure enough to approach someone, much less start up a conversation. Sammy's board of directors was made up of the following people:

Albert Einstein

Leonardo da Vinci

Julia Roberts

Donald Trump

Lance Armstrong

Merlin, the magician of the Arthurian legend

When I asked Sammy to describe how he was like any of these people, he responded, "Well, I'm smart like Einstein, and I'm athletic like Lance Armstrong, who amazes me with his drive. I admire 'the Donald' for how he's made something of himself. I like to think of myself as a little bit of an artist, which is why I thought of da Vinci."

I asked Sammy why he listed Julia Roberts and Merlin. At first he was a little stumped, but after a few moments of reflection he said, "It's not so much that I'm like them, but there's something really interesting about them. I mean, Julia Roberts is just about the most beautiful woman in the world, yet she's always so easygoing and natural. And I've always liked the character of Merlin; he's a magician and he can make things happen."

I asked Sammy to ponder images of Julia and Merlin in his mind's eye to see what beliefs he had about them. I asked him, "What parts of their personalities would you like to incorporate into your own behavior?" Sammy was quick to respond, "Well, I'd like to be natural and easygoing and I'd like to have a little bit of magic in my life."

I asked Sammy if he could visualize in his mind his personal board of directors sitting around his dinner table and having a conversation with each one of them. He responded, "Yes, and they're all telling me it's okay to be me. They're like my own team of cheerleaders!" Sammy saw that his board of directors was his inner support system. With practice, Sammy learned that whenever he felt alone, isolated, or overcome by doubt, all he had to do was call forth his personal board.

Sammy also found that he could send his board before him to any social situations he was about to enter. So when he entered a social situation, he pictured, to the full extent of his imagination, his confidence team being with him. As a result, he felt easygoing, relaxed, and smart, and his renewed confidence allowed him to more easily talk with women.

Meeting Your Inner Confidence Coach

In chapter 1 you identified your inner critic, giving it a name and an image. You've just met your personal board of directors, who are part of your confidence team. But all teams need a coach or adviser to coordinate, motivate, and guide them.

Martin Rossman (2000) states that almost all major philosophical, religious, and psychological traditions include inner personal guidance in one form or another. Different cultures around the world have used prayer, meditation, chanting, fasting, dancing, and music to tap into this inner source of wisdom, which may also be referred to as an "inner healer," the "still, small voice in our mind," "guardian angel," or "inner adviser." We all have an internal resource that is compassionate, wise, and loving. This inner confidence coach is readily available to you at all times.

Your inner coach may be a character from a movie, or it could be an animal or a combination of people from your past and your imagination. This coach may appear as a wise, loving old man or wise old woman who looks remarkably like an older version of you. He or she may be real or imaginary, alive or dead, or appear as a special animal, plant, or natural force such as the wind or sun. Your coach may even show itself as a compassionate religious figure like Jesus, Buddha, or Moses.

Just like an athletic coach, your inner confidence coach will help you solve problems, get a winning attitude, believe in yourself, and help you behave with confidence. This important figure can assist you in learning to understand yourself and can act as a source of deep support and comfort.

Let's now meet your inner confidence coach.

Guided Imagery Exercise #3

1. *Take the phone off the hook and do whatever you can to create a quiet space for the next twenty minutes. Sit in a comfortable chair, with your feet flat on the floor, and allow yourself to relax. Kick off your shoes and loosen any tight clothing or belts.*

2. *Close your eyes and know that you are perfectly safe. Begin to take some slow, deep breaths.*

   Breathe slowly and deeply, your belly rising and falling. Inhale . . . and exhale. Inhale . . . and exhale. Inhale . . . and exhale. Let the stress of the day melt away. When you sense an inner calm-

ness and relaxation, you'll find that your body is relaxing with each breath. You are safe, protected, and alert.

3. *In this relaxed state, allow an image to come to your mind that represents your personal place, which you first visited in guided imagery exercise 1. By now, you should know this place well. As you sit and relax in your personal place, know that something good is about to appear.*

4. *Look around your personal place and make eye contact with the first living creature you see. Smile at this presence and welcome it. You may ask the being to come closer to you. You may even reach over and touch it. When you have the sense that this presence is a wise and supportive being that has your best interests at heart, ask it if it will be your confidence coach.*

5. *Allow yourself to commune with this presence, and ask its name. Ask any questions you might have and let your confidence coach respond in a way you understand. Quietly hold the answers in your mind.*

6. *Ask your confidence coach if it will be with you in the future whenever you need support in being confident. When you feel ready, thank your confidence coach for all its love, support, and wisdom. When it seems like the appropriate time, you can say good-bye.*

7. *Begin to leave your personal place in whatever way feels most comfortable to you. You may wiggle your fingers and toes, and, as you come back to full awareness in your chair, you will know that you're at peace, refreshed and energized.*

8. *Slowly open your eyes. When you are ready, write about this guided imagery experience and your confidence coach in your notebook.*

Finding Your Own Confidence Style

It's in our nature as humans to dwell on failures and not always on successes. Yet, as you reclaim your confidence and allow your board of directors and inner confidence coach to guide your ABCs of self-confidence, you'll start adopting a belief that you are capable of accomplishing your goals. Don't focus on what you don't have or can't do, but rather focus on what you do have and what you can do! When you do this, you'll be gaining control of your life rather than being at the mercy of negative beliefs, bad attitudes, and self-defeating behaviors. With this new awareness you'll also find yourself becoming more attuned to the hidden metaphors that your confidence coach brings to you, and you'll start to develop your own confidence style.

THE HIDDEN METAPHORS IN YOUR CONFIDENCE COACH

My inner confidence coach is Apollo, the Roman mythological god of light and healing. Sometimes viewed as the Roman god of the sun, Apollo represents order, harmony, and reason. Apollo is seen as having the power to ward off evil and darkness. He's considered the patron god of wisdom and has the power of the morning sun.

For many years, my childhood experience of being trapped in a locked freezer caused me to be fearful of exploring new opportunities and places. Whenever I felt trapped or backed into a corner, I would freeze. I held the constant belief that exploring the world would get me in trouble, and that I wouldn't be able to handle the consequences, whatever they might be. So, even though I wanted to try new things or get out of bad situations, I was often stuck.

With some reflection, I was not surprised to discover that Apollo could easily light my way out of any dark freezer and dispel any self-doubt about being able to get out of a tight space. As I reflected on what Apollo meant to me and the metaphors that this image brought forth, I suddenly recalled how enthralled I was as a young boy with NASA's Project Apollo, which sent astronauts to the moon. Talk about exploring new adventures! It was clear that Apollo was my inner confidence coach.

Visual images speak to us all in metaphors and symbols. Apollo, with his power of sunlight and wisdom, is an archetypal figure full of hidden meaning and metaphors. Apollo's strength assures me that all is well. Susan's inner confidence coach is named Miss Breezy, a confident woman wearing a summer sundress, free of the strict confines that bind Lady Constriction. For John, a bald eagle, a symbol of strength in the Native American tradition, sends Chief Rain Cloud on his way.

SUNSHINE CONFIDENCE

A longtime friend of mine taught me the importance of finding my own style of confidence. Bob was always very sure of himself and could handle just about any situation confidently. Whenever I tried to figure out how to act in a situation I would ask Bob how he thought I should act. Bob would effortlessly lay out a plan for me, with lots of details and even the words to say. When I found myself in a self-doubting situation, I would try to copy his style of being confident. Yet each time I tried to "be Bob," my efforts fell flat.

What was I doing wrong? I had memorized the words and phrases, and I'd even figured out how to mimic his voice tone, inflection, and facial gestures. What I finally realized, however, is that I was operating from Bob's style and not my own. I wasn't speaking or acting authentically from my own confidence style because I believed my own style wasn't good enough.

You have a personal confidence style. It may be easygoing, sunny, or slow and deliberate. The next guided imagery exercise will help you discover or rediscover your unique style. You'll recognize the first part of this exercise; you are now becoming very adept at entering into a deep relaxed state conducive to visualization and guided imagery.

Guided Imagery Exercise #4

1. *Take the phone off the hook and do whatever you can to create a quiet space for the next twenty minutes. Sit in a comfortable chair, with your feet flat on the floor, and allow yourself to relax. Kick off your shoes and loosen any tight clothing or belts.*

2. *Close your eyes and know that you are perfectly safe. Begin to take some slow, deep breaths.*

    Breathe slowly and deeply, your belly rising and falling. Inhale . . . and exhale. Inhale . . . and exhale. Inhale . . . and exhale. Let the stress of the day melt away. When you sense an inner calmness and relaxation, you'll find that your body is relaxing with each breath. You are safe, protected, and alert.

3. *While paying attention to your breathing, now begin to imagine a ball of clear light hanging directly over your head, bathing you in a warm glow. This light feels so good and warm, and you know that with each ray caressing your body you're protected and nourished.*

4. *As you feel this clear, clean, warm light slowly flowing over your body, you begin to notice your scalp and forehead relax. Your face relaxes,*

your neck and shoulders drop, your chest feels warm, and your deep breathing gets deeper and deeper.

5. *As the warm, protective light flows down your chest and into your belly, your whole torso begins to relax. The light continues down your hips, your thighs, and your legs. Finally, as it relaxes your feet, the warm light drains out of the bottom of your feet all the way down deep into the earth.*

6. *You're now deeply relaxed, safe, and secure. Allow yourself to imagine your personal place and allow your inner confidence coach to appear before you. Your coach is compassionate and supportive, and you can feel this with great intensity.*

7. *With your inner confidence coach as a guide, allow yourself to remember a situation in which you were confident. Where were you? What were you doing? How were you dressed and what were you saying? Can you recall any special sounds or colors from that day? What time was it? Were there other people around? Allow yourself to vividly remember this time and how good it felt to be confident.*

8. *Allow yourself to imagine a symbol of this confident time—a symbol that represents all the feelings and beliefs about this special moment in your life.*

9. *When you are ready, and you know you can bring this confidence back with you in some form, allow the feelings and images to fade. You can say good-bye to your personal place and inner confidence coach for now. Thank your coach for being with you and for helping you remember a time when you were supremely confident.*

10. *Now bring that sense of confidence back to the present time and place. Take a few energizing breaths, wiggle your toes and fingers, and begin*

to stretch your body. When you're ready, slowly open your eyes, feeling perhaps more confident than when you first began.

11. *Fully awake, tell yourself that you can return to this personal place and bring to mind your confidence coach whenever you want by simply imagining in your mind's eye how it feels. Tell yourself that you can recall the feelings and images of being confident whenever you want. Remind yourself that each and every time you encounter a stress- or doubt-filled situation, your inner confidence coach will be there to help you remember your confidence style.*

12. *In your notebook, write about the images and metaphors that came to you as you conducted this exercise. These images represent your confidence style. See if you can find a photograph or an image representing your confidence symbol and style. This symbol is always with you.*

The Big Picture

In this chapter you've learned that your beliefs determine your self-image. You've identified your personal board of directors, met your inner confidence coach, and explored your unique confidence style. Now that you've made these important tools and inner resources available to yourself, let's move forward to choose the behavior you'd like to focus on—for example, you can choose to focus on developing self-confidence for speaking in public, asking for a raise, or going on a first date.

4

choosing what to focus on

"As I lay there thinking of my vision, I could see it all again and feel the meaning with a part of me like a strange power glowing in my body." —Black Elk

Black Elk's quote, above, speaks eloquently to the power of imagery. When you feel your desired outcome with great intensity, you're actively participating in strengthening your attitude and confidence to act in accordance with your imagination. You may have identified several situations in your life where you want to apply newfound confidence, but for now let's pick one area.

Making the Choice to Improve Your Self-Confidence

Every day you're presented with opportunities to make choices about your self-confidence. Choices can be a repeat of the previous day's choices or they can be a chance to reach new levels of success and confidence. Every day you can choose to continue pedaling a stationary bike that goes nowhere and remain in your familiar comfort zone. Or you can make new choices, set new goals, and imagine a new vision of a self-confident future. When you arrive at a place in life where you are ready to commit to doing it differently, you're taking a vital step. By making new choices, you're ready to focus on your future and not on your past.

However, a choice that isn't clearly defined remains an ethereal wisp of thin air. Have you ever had a vision that drifted in and out of your consciousness yet remained sitting on a shelf, gathering dust, without ever being realized? Without being clearly defined, these faint visions don't have the power to motivate you. More important, they don't provide you with a road map that would show you how to get from point A to point B.

When this happens, you're neither here nor there; you're stuck in murky waters constantly treading water. Sometimes we remain stuck in just such an in-between place for months and even years. This isn't a fun or comfortable place to be. So let's get unstuck and choose new goals to be more confident, and to more confidently align your new attitudes and beliefs with new behaviors. This chapter will help you do just that.

WHAT YOU'VE LEARNED SO FAR

All of the steps you've taken and exercises you've done up to now have set the stage for you to be more confident. You've learned that guided imagery is a powerful tool that allows you to prepare, practice, and anticipate the reality of being confident and self-assured. You've discovered that guided imagery can train your body and mind to appear before large crowds, engage in difficult conversations, meet daily goals, take risks, and make forward strides at work.

You've learned that guided imagery can help you anticipate the adrenaline rush that comes with false expectations appearing real and can quiet your anxiety so that you don't panic and run. Whether it's the adrenaline rush of walking up to a stranger at a party to start a conversation, or learning new skills at work to increase your value, you've mentally rehearsed new beliefs and attitudes so that you can tackle these situations confidently. You've also found out that by returning to your personal place on a regular basis and calling upon your inner confidence coach, you can quiet your inner critic and confidently execute your desired behaviors.

Still, making these new choices to improve your confidence may come with feelings of apprehension. These feelings may arise because making choices to live more confidently creates change in your life.

CHANGE IS GREAT AS LONG AS EVERYTHING STAYS THE SAME

Over the years I've heard many people say that they love change. People will describe change as stimulating, invigorating, thrilling, adventurous, and exciting. Perhaps they've been to a weekend conference to acquire new skills and now they're filled with excitement and ready to take on the world, or maybe they're starting a new chapter in their life. I've also discovered, however, that when it comes right down to it most of us only "love" change as long as everything stays the same.

Helen Harkness, career consultant and coach, puts it simply: "Change, for most people, is essentially a four-letter word" (1997, 45). So why do we maintain the status quo? It's because change brings with it the unknown, and the unknown may prompt us to incorrectly believe the false evidence appearing real. However, as you've learned, this isn't true.

Along with the unknown, you may need to leave behind something that has perhaps been familiar to you for a long time: the Ogre of Self-Doubt. You still might find yourself clinging to old behaviors and old beliefs because they're comfortable and familiar. But this resistance to change doesn't have to short-circuit all the progress you've made so far.

RESISTANCE

In psychology, the term "resistance" refers to the barriers to progress we create when we seek change but keep "treading water" despite our good intentions. You may have experienced your own attitudinal resistance if you've let things get in the way of your daily imagery practice. You may have experienced resistance if you let your inner critic convince you that all your good work is just plain silly and a waste of time. You may have discovered behavioral resistance when you've gained valuable new insights but haven't put your insight into action. You might become so frustrated that you give up. Please don't give up.

It's Okay to Feel Resistance

If you've felt resistance at this point, it's okay. Resistance to change is to be expected. Don't beat yourself up. If your inner critic pounces on you, find a quiet space and use the beginnings of the guided imagery script you've become familiar with in the earlier guided imagery exercises. Call on your inner confidence coach. In doing so, you're practicing the ABCs of confidence and reinforcing a new confident self-image. After a while you'll believe and use the positive support that your confidence coach offers. Remember, making any change requires effort on your part, and as you become more accustomed to and skilled in using guided imagery you'll also become more and more confident.

Choose an Area to Focus On

People often tell me they want to develop confidence in all areas of their life, and that there are so many things they want to try that they can't pick just one. When I hear this I know that this is a form of resistance. They focus on how many things they want to change and in essence end up not choosing anything at all. Consequently they remain stuck. I then suggest, "For the time being, let's pick just one area to focus on."

For the purposes of this chapter and the remainder of this book, I invite you to choose one area of your life in which you want to develop confidence. Perhaps you want to increase your confidence in your professional life: interviewing for a new job, asking for a raise, learning new skills, or giving a public presentation. Or you might want to focus on confidence in your personal life: dating again after a divorce or breakup, beginning or maintaining an exercise program, moving to a new city, returning to school, or learning how to bungee jump. For now, pick one area that seems realistic and manageable. Remember, after you've practiced all the exercises in this book while focusing on that one area, you can apply what you've learned to any area of your life.

Awareness Exercise #7

1. To help you focus, begin a new page in your notebook and write the first things that come to your mind when you answer the following questions (take it easy now—not too many):

    - What would you do if you knew you absolutely could not or would not fail?

    - How could you make your life more fun?

    - When are you most at peace?

    - What new adventures do you want to explore?

    - What dream have you been putting off year after year?

    Your answers to these questions will help you choose what to focus on. Your answers might look something like the following:

    - I'd start my own business.

    - I'd go dancing.

    - I'd learn something new each and every day.

    - I'm most at peace while baking holiday cookies as gifts.

- I'd travel to Italy.

- I'd start writing my great American novel.

2. Take a look at your answers and see if anything comes to you. Now, in your notebook, turn to a fresh page and complete the following sentence:

I choose to focus on _____.

A MIDLIFE CAREER CHOICE

Cathy first came to my university coaching class looking for the confidence to make a career change. Now in her early fifties, Cathy had worked in corporate telephone sales for over twenty years. She felt she didn't have the confidence to start a more meaningful career. Balancing her own life, caring for her elderly mother, and planning her daughter's wedding, she felt that life had somehow passed her by. She had no time for herself. I assured her that even while continuing to honor her family obligations, she could find the confidence to nurture herself and her vision of a fulfilling career.

I asked Cathy to imagine a time in life when she was most at peace, where she was doing something just for herself. After a few moments of reflection she said, "When I'm baking cookies. I can see myself getting up early in the morning, and I love the warm smells of baking filling my house. It's a quiet, calm time for me, and I'm very much at peace. And I love to see the looks on people's faces as they taste these goodies, especially around the holidays." Cathy then added, "But this doesn't really mean anything, does it? And besides, I don't have the slightest idea of how to make sense of any of this."

I asked Cathy what she would do if she knew she could absolutely not fail. She responded, "I'd become a master pastry chef." Next, I asked her how she could have more fun in her life, and she replied, "I'd take a chance and do what I've always wanted to do." When I asked her to imagine a new, confident image of herself, she described herself "traveling to cooking schools all over the world and learning from the best chefs." Last, I asked Cathy to describe what dreams she had found herself putting off year after year. With no hesitation whatsoever Cathy looked at me and said, "Being a pastry chef."

With these answers in hand, Cathy was ready to do a fun and creative focus assignment. In fact, it's the very same awareness exercise that you're about to do. This exercise doesn't take very long, but it does require your focused attention.

Creating Your Vision Board

Creating a picture vision board is a wonderful way to help you identify areas of your life you'd like to focus on. Sometimes described as a treasure map or road map to success, a vision board holds all kinds of interesting, subtle, yet profound clues. I've used vision boards while working with both children and adults and have found them to be an effective means to discover or rediscover dreams as well as unlock innate creativity.

You've probably heard the cliché "If you don't have a map to show you how to get to where you want to go, you'll probably end up someplace you don't want to be." Your vision board will help you recognize the road that you're taking and keep you on track.

Creating your vision board is a great stress buster. You'll be surprised at how calm and joyful you feel when you finish this exercise. If your inner critic shows up to say, "This is just fun and games," gently call on your inner confidence coach for support and allow yourself the opportunity to fully benefit from bringing your positive visions to life. Most important, enjoy this process.

Before you start, gather an assortment of magazines. That stack of magazines that you've been meaning to recycle will be perfect. You may even want to ask your friends and neighbors for their old magazines so you'll have a variety. Collect as many different kinds of magazines as you can. Don't be concerned about whether they're sports, fitness, automobile, news, house and garden, gossip, or lifestyle magazines. Any and all magazines that have pictures will be just fine. You're now ready to create your vision board for confidence and success.

Awareness Exercise #8

1. Without thinking, flip through the magazines and, when an image strikes you as interesting, tear it out. You don't have to consciously understand why the image is appealing to you; just act on your instincts here. It's best to do this in one sitting if you can, but if this isn't convenient, it's okay to take two or three days to complete your vision board. It doesn't matter how many images you have for your board. I've seen some vision boards crammed full with overlapping images. I've also seen some vision boards with only a small handful of images, perhaps five or six. I've even seen a few vision boards with only one image. It doesn't matter how many or how few images you have, as long as each and every one of them is deeply meaningful to you.

You may find words in magazines that attract your attention as well. If so, that's okay, but try not to use too many words. The idea here is that a picture is worth a thousand words, remember?

After you've finished cutting out all the images and photographs that appeal to you, set them aside.

2. Make a visit to your local art or craft store. If you've never been in an art store, you're in for a nice adventure. You'll find lots of colorful items, calligraphy pens, highlighters, stickers, and many tools for exercising your creative imagination. Purchase a large colored poster board, the kind that children use for their school projects. Choose a color that you are instinctively drawn to. It could be a robust red for passion, a sunburst yellow for personal power, a deep purple or blue, or a soothing green. If you want to choose black or white, that's okay too. Choose whatever color you want. This will become the background for your vision board.

3. When you return home, place your poster board on a flat surface in a room where you won't be interrupted. Make sure you have a comfortable place to sit. With glue or tape, begin to secure your magazine images and clippings onto your colored board. Enjoy the process of intuitively placing your images where you want them, working with the colors, textures, feelings, juxtapositions, and meaningful images.

4. Once you've assembled your vision board, place it where you can see it each and every day, preferably so it's the

last thing you see in the evening before going to sleep and the first thing you see in the morning as you wake up. Even the bathroom is okay! If you like, you can make your vision board three-dimensional. Mark, an advertising executive who wanted to start his own business, made his vision board into a mobile. He attached a string to it and hung it over his bed. Truly, his vision board was the first and last thing he saw each and every day.

5. As you live with your vision board, imagine it's on the front page of your morning newspaper, with a headline running underneath it. Imagine what the headline would be. It could be something like "Supreme Confidence" or "Living an Artful Life." Let a headline come to you naturally. Mark's headline was "Flying High." The headline you come up with is now the title of your vision board and your motto for moving forward with confidence in life.

REFLECTING ON YOUR VISION

Over the next several days, as you live with your completed vision board, reflect on its presence and meaning. Mull over how the images and patterns are arranged. Can you see themes starting to reveal themselves? Do you see any concrete, forward-moving steps emerging? Your vision board can help you focus on what's important for you. If you feel comfortable, share it with friends, family members, or a therapist and ask what they see. But if for any reason you feel that others in your life won't be supportive of your new vision of yourself, then by all means protect your vision from outside critics.

PROTECTING YOUR VISION

Joan, a former coaching client of mine, felt no one would support her new future vision of a new job. She didn't feel comfortable displaying her board at home for fear of ridicule or criticism, so she put the board in her car trunk, knowing that it was safe and sound. It went everywhere with her. Then Joan decided to make a more-portable vision board and found duplicate images. She pasted the mini-vision onto two adjoining pages in her notebook. When she went to interview for new jobs, she held her notebook open in front of her as if she were taking notes. This way she was able to glance at her vision board during the interview, keeping her goals fully in her sight.

Having her vision board visible during interviews helped Joan maintain her confidence, keep focused on her strengths, and remain calm. While talking with potential employers, she could measure the new job against the vision she held of her future success. She knew immediately when it did or didn't match up. Her feelings would speak loud and clear when the experience of learning about the new job wasn't congruent with the vision she had meticulously created on her vision board.

INTERPRETING YOUR VISION

Cathy's vision board included many overlapping images of white picket fences and open doors of all sorts: doors and more doors, all opening. Next to these door images she had placed images of pies, cookies, and brownies. As Cathy and I sat together deciphering the images on her vision board, it became crystal clear to us that her vision was indeed to pursue a career as a pastry chef. I asked Cathy not to let too many logistical issues prevent her from exploring how she might go about this, at least for the time being. I encouraged her to instead gently do some research into how she could pursue a career in baking. Cathy titled her vision board "New Doors Opening."

Cathy searched the Web for culinary schools, talked to people who were already employed in the field, and allowed herself to simply explore possibilities of how this dream might become a reality. After some time, when she had gathered all the relevant information she needed, she came to the decision to apply to the Culinary Institute of America (CIA) in Northern California.

Cathy was accepted at the CIA, attended the program, and graduated. When she returned to Southern California, she landed her first paying job as a pastry chef in one of the top local restaurants. How did she do it? Well, when Cathy imagined herself at peace, focused on her vision, and gained the confidence to live her dreams, her vision came true. The same can happen for you.

The last time I saw Cathy, she was working in a favorite restaurant of mine, with baking powder dusting her face. She had begun living her vision. She was confident and happy.

LIVING WITH YOUR VISION

As you live with your vision board, allow the images and emerging feelings to seep into your consciousness. In doing so, you're exercising your mental muscles, creating a mental fitness plan for your future, and training your mind to respond appropriately. Your vision declares what's important to you. It's poetic, visceral, imaginative, and feeling based—a spiritual promise of a new quality of life. Ultimately your vision board gives you permission to imagine yourself at your confident best.

Reflect on your vision board daily, focusing your attention on where you want to go in life. When you do this, your creative juices will start to turn on, and your ABCs will begin to line up. With your clearly focused vision, you'll start to feel a greater sense of personal power. Your subconscious will become your friend and ally, as it plants the seeds for your future growth; it becomes the fertile soil that nurtures your seedlings, allowing them to thrive on the positive energy you give them.

COMMITTING TO YOUR VISION

When you start to live with your vision every day, you're committing to making it a reality, and your future begins to unfold. As you move from passive powerlessness to confidence, your vision, nurtured by your personal truths, values, and strengths, grows stronger each day. Combined with the connection and awareness you've been accumulating in this book, your vision becomes a magnetic field that attracts all sorts of wonderful happenings. As the cornerstone of your personal power, your vision moves you beyond the past, beyond the present, to grasp the bigger picture of your future. With your focused and clear vision as a guide, you'll begin to see and understand intuitively where you want to go and what choices you want to make. Your commitment to follow an action plan (which we'll discuss in greater depth in the next chapter) begins to glow brightly.

I'm reminded of one of my favorite quotes, which speaks to the power of commitment in following a vision. William Hutchinson Murray (1913–96) was one of the great Scottish mountaineering explorers who popularized Scotland as a destination for walking and climbing. A World War II prisoner of war, he eventually became a member of the 1950 Scottish Himalayan expedition. Sadly, weakened by his wartime prisoner experiences, he was prevented from taking part in the successful 1953 Mount Everest expedition led by Sir Edmund Hillary. Nonetheless, Murray's writings, including those in his book *The Scottish Himalayan Expedition* (1951), have inspired many to seek confidence in their lives. Here is my favorite:

> *Until one is committed there is hesitancy, the chance to draw back, always ineffectiveness. Concerning all acts of initiative or creation, there is one elementary truth, the ignorance of which kills countless ideas and splendid plans: That the moment one definitely commits oneself, then Providence moves too.*
>
> *All sorts of things occur to help one that would never otherwise have occurred. A whole stream of events issues from the decision, raising in one's favor all manner of unforeseen incidents and meetings and material assistance, which no man could have dreamt would have come his way.*
>
> *I have learned a deep respect for one of Goethe's couplets: Whatever you can do, or dream you can, begin it. Boldness has genius, power, and magic in it.*

Before we close this chapter, let's return to a guided imagery script to anchor your vision into your awareness. You'll recognize the opening parts of the following exercise, since you're already familiar with the process of entering into a deep relaxed state.

Guided Imagery Exercise #5

1. *Take the phone off the hook and do whatever you can to create a quiet space for the next twenty minutes. Sit in a comfortable chair, with your feet flat on the floor, and allow yourself to relax. Kick off your shoes and loosen any tight clothing or belts.*

2. *Close your eyes and know that you are perfectly safe. Begin to take some slow, deep breaths.*

   Breathe slowly and deeply, your belly rising and falling. Inhale . . . and exhale. Inhale . . . and exhale. Inhale . . . and exhale. Let the stress of the day melt away. When you sense an inner calmness and relaxation, you'll find that your body is relaxing with each breath. You are safe, protected, and alert.

3. *While paying attention to your breathing, now begin to imagine a ball of clear light hanging directly over your head, bathing you in a warm glow. This light feels so good and warm, and you know that with each ray you're protected and nourished.*

4. *As you feel this clear, clean, warm light slowly flowing over your body, you begin to notice your scalp and forehead relax. Your face relaxes, your neck and shoulders drop, your chest feels warm, and your deep breathing gets deeper and deeper.*

5. *As the warm, protective light flows down your chest and into your belly, it too begins to relax. The light continues down your hips, your thighs, and your legs. Finally, as it relaxes your feet, the warm light drains out of the bottom of your feet all the way down deep into the earth.*

6. *You're now deeply relaxed, safe, and secure. Imagine returning to your personal place. Remember how good it feels to be here, safe and secure.*

7. *While in your personal place, allow yourself to imagine your vision board in front of you. Imagine that your vision board is coming to life. Imagine that you are sitting in a movie theater, and the scenes from your vision board are playing out one after another. In the scenes, where are you? Are there other people around? If so, who? What time of day is it? How are you dressed? What are you doing?*

8. *While deeply sensing your vision coming to life, project yourself into the movie as being strong and on top of the world, imagining yourself confident and living your life fully.*

9. *When you are ready, you can allow the feelings and images to fade. You can say good-bye to your personal place for now and slowly begin to come back to the present time and place. Take a few energizing breaths, wiggle your toes and fingers, and begin to stretch your body.*

   When you're ready, slowly open your eyes, feeling refreshed, happy, and calm.

10. *Fully awake, tell yourself that you can return to this personal place whenever you want, by simply imagining in your mind's eye how good it feels. Tell yourself that you can recall all the feelings and images of being confident and can call on them whenever you want.*

The Big Picture

This chapter has helped you make a choice about what to focus on. Joan made a simple choice to focus on developing the confidence to interview for new jobs, and to protect her vision. She chose to keep her vision close to herself so it couldn't be trampled on by others. Cathy made the choice to explore new options. More important, she made the choice to explore new options without listening to her inner critic's harsh judgments, such as "This is crazy. You can't be a professional chef. You should stick with what you know!" Cathy made a simple choice not to listen to her inner critic anymore if it meant her vision of the future would be crushed. It was as simple as that—making a choice to focus on her future, not on her past.

You've also learned in this chapter that resistance is to be expected. Resistance is okay. Just noticing the resistance that comes up will help you move through it and keep on track. You've had an enjoyable time creating your vision board, and each day as you live with your vision you're finding yourself more and more confident. When you're focused on your vision and are committed to making it a reality, the unseen hand of Providence starts to move. Before you move forward to the next chapter to learn how small changes can have enormous impacts, turn to a fresh page in your notebook and complete this sentence:

Today I choose to focus on _____.

5

the big impact of small changes

"Where thought goes, chi follows." —Chinese proverb

Take a few moments and imagine, in your mind's eye, a tiny pebble dropping into a pool of water. As you imagine this pebble falling into the water, you begin to sense ripples extending outward. Imagine that this pebble has fallen into the deep blue ocean, and the ripples continue on for miles and miles. Now imagine you're standing on the shore of a great ocean and a small wave laps up against your feet. The pebble that was dropped in the middle of the ocean has caused this wave to travel thousands of miles and is the very same wave that is now touching your feet. It's true: small changes can have big impacts.

Whatever You Focus On Becomes Magnified

The ancient Chinese proverb above brings to mind the importance of the small things in life. Chi is a fundamental concept in Chinese culture and medicine, and it is most often defined as "air" or "breath." Accordingly, chi is the life force or spiritual energy that is a part of everything that exists. A subtle form of energy, this life force is believed to permeate the body and mind. The concept of chi began entering Western culture in the 1970s through the rise in popularity of martial arts and bears a great deal of similarity to the fictional Jedi "Force" in George Lucas's *Star Wars* films. Chi is a wonderful, essential tool that can bring us closer to the life we were meant to live.

If you accept and use your life force as a source of strength, then you'll find your confidence increasing. But if you allow yourself to continue focusing on self-defeating beliefs and a negative self-image, your life force will be defeated. If you don't focus positive energy on the vision you created for yourself in the previous chapter, you'll continue creating self-fulfilling prophecies of self-doubt. By now, you've learned how imperative it is to consciously, purposefully, and actively direct your mental positive imagery forward, believing in your own vision of strong self-confidence and engaging in the daily practice of life-affirming guided imagery.

WHAT AM I DOING WRONG?

Lao-tzu, a Chinese philosopher from the sixth century B.C. and a contemporary of Confucius, is credited with saying, "The journey of a thousand miles begins with one step." Never have wiser words been spoken!

"But what am I missing?" I'm sometimes asked. "I've used the guided imagery awareness scripts every day, I reflect on my vision board in the morning and in the evening, and yet my vision still hasn't come true." When I encounter this question, I reply, "You only need to take one step each day. What are you doing each and every day to bring yourself one step closer to your vision?"

This question usually sparks eager responses relating all sorts of good, positive steps people are taking each and every day. This is great! Then somewhere toward the end of a sentence, as the person's voice trails off, I hear, "But, you know, I really can't make the changes I want to make. How would I support myself? I can't move my family or quit my job. I have responsibilities!"

Ah! The stumbling blocks revealed. While I would never advise anyone to quit his or her job on a whim, or do something that is otherwise out of character, I do suggest that the willingness to be open to change and take small, incremental steps is a key ingredient in achieving one's vision.

WILLINGNESS

In his book *You'll See It When You Believe It* (2001, 53), Wayne Dyer beautifully describes the importance of willingness: "You need to examine how willing you are to do what it takes to make your dream a reality. . . . Willingness is really a state of mind. It is an internal statement that says 'I will be happiness and bring it to my undertakings.'"

Being open to willingness doesn't mean that you need to push yourself into uncharacteristic behavior, selling all your worldly possessions and leaving your family. What it does mean, however, is that you're willing to consider fresh new possibilities that haven't been revealed to you yet or that you haven't previously considered. It's about being open to being open. Being willing brings you to a point where the power of creative imagination moves into and through your life.

If you imagine yourself as being full of self-doubt, you're reinforcing the negative ABCs of confidence, and eventually the self-doubt will become true. For this reason, it's crucial to keep positive images in your mind, even if you encounter obstacles. Certainly there will be occasional setbacks and disappointments, but if you allow images of self-confidence to be the dominant images in your mind you'll find yourself wanting to do things that reinforce continual improvement. As Dyer (2001) says, if you imagine yourself poor you'll act on this belief every day. You'll think poor thoughts, your body will slump, you'll be depressed and feel overwhelmed, and your behavior, beliefs, and attitudes will continually reinforce this.

What are you willing to do? Are you willing to take one step each day? Dyer writes, "Forget about determination, personal drive, and will power. These don't help with imagery. You must be willing to do what it takes" (2001, 52). To do what it takes doesn't mean you have to give up everything and live like a homeless person. Rather, to do what it takes may mean that you stretch your mental ability to grow, much like a fitness coach motivates you to move past your comfort zone. Once you're willing and your vision is clear, your actions will be clear too. Make sure your vision of confidence is really your own vision. Remember that there are no failures. There are no mistakes. There are only results and opportunities for growth and improvement.

BABY STEPS, BABY STEPS, BABY STEPS

The best way to understand small, incremental steps is to watch a young child learn to walk. As we all know, before children can run they first have to learn how to walk. Before they can learn to walk, they have to learn how to stand up. Before they can stand up, they have to learn how to crawl, and before they can crawl they have to learn to roll over. Each step along the way builds upon itself, ultimately leading to the goal of walking. A child's first step is built upon daily trials and practice. Indeed, small steps can and do have a big impact.

The Japanese Way of Kaizen

Robert Maurer is the director of behavioral sciences for the Family Practice Residency Program at UCLA Medical Center and a faculty member of the UCLA School of Medicine. In his book *One Small Step Can Change Your Life: The Kaizen Way* (2004), he explores the concept of *kaizen*, a Japanese term that means "continuous improvement." He reminds us that small changes don't have to be radical or revolutionary. Like a child learning to walk, you can benefit from making small changes as well. Gentle, small actions will circumvent the nagging voice of your inner critic, quiet the bodily sensation of the fight-or-flight mechanism, and propel you toward continuous improvement each and every day.

You just need to remember the following:

- Break it down into bite-sized pieces.

- You don't need to do it all at once.

- Simply be consistent with your daily practice.

Small Daily Successes

Confidence grows when you experience small daily successes. These successes are rewards in and of themselves, and with each passing day they add up to larger successes. A pat on the back for a job well done or a simple compliment will boost anyone's confidence level, including your own. Give yourself these pats on the back. You'll begin to feel your confidence growing each and every day. Smile, stand tall, make eye contact with people, imagine your confidence coach standing right behind you, and adopt the body posture and body language of a confident person. You are self-confident, and taking small daily steps will only breed more success.

The cliché is true: whatever you focus on increases! Focus on the small steps, and the big steps will take care of themselves. Firmly believe in your full potential and your confidence will grow daily.

Awareness Exercise #9

What small daily success have you had since you began this book? List in your notebook three small successes that have an impact on your confidence:

1. _____

2. _____

3. _____

Below are some examples of small successes:

I regularly practice good self-care, and I feel calmer and more relaxed.

I'm not so afraid to speak up in meetings at work.

I can introduce myself to new people.

I don't toss and turn every night worrying about things I said during the day.

KEEPING YOUR EYE ON THE BIG PICTURE

With time and many baby steps, you're gradually able to take slightly larger steps toward reaching your confidence goal. Eventually the day arrives when you sense you're making greater progress as your steps become grouped together in meaningful ways. For example, if your confidence goal is to return to graduate school, your baby steps might have included researching degree requirements, researching college Web sites, visiting various schools, meeting with academic advisers, identifying prerequisites, taking community classes to address any deficient areas on your transcript, talking to alumni, securing financial aid, applying to your preferred graduate schools, getting accepted into a program, and signing up for classes on your first day as a graduate student! The first semester turns into the second semester, and then the third, and before you know it, you're graduating, sheepskin in hand. You've accomplished your goal by making very practical choices! Take a moment to list in your notebook ten baby steps that you can commit to so you can accomplish your goal.

Awareness Exercise #10

1. First, list your confidence goal below:

    I will or I want _____.

2. In order to accomplish this goal, I will take the following baby steps:

_____

_____

_____

_____

_____

_____

_____

_____

_____

_____

Congratulations! You're making excellent progress. Give yourself a pat on the back for all your hard work. See how easy it is to make progress without having to suffer?

You Don't Need to Suffer to Grow

Rob came to me for coaching while in a career transition. Rob's inner critic, nicknamed "the Brat," was a precocious yet impetuous child with a mean streak and a foul mouth. His inner confidence coach was named Esther West, a woman who had helped his mom with chores around the house when he and his sister were growing up. Esther had always been a great inspiration to Rob and remained one of the most important people in his life, even though she had passed on a few years before. Rob described Esther as "a symbol of serenity and encouragement, and the epitome of love and compassion. She makes me feel confident."

Making the transition from running his own advertising and public relations company to managing the family business, Rob found that a simple shift in the image he was focusing on (from the Brat to Esther) was powerful. "Maybe it's just to take a single breath, or to take two minutes to walk outside. These acts change my whole day and my outlook." For Rob, other simple rituals included boiling hot water in a kettle, making and then enjoying a cup of tea, and "tearing off the sticky adhesive paper and putting on a fresh pair of new socks." These small actions made him happy, more relaxed, centered, and ready to take on the world.

Katie, a single mom of three who had gone through a painful divorce, found it important to remember the following truth: "I'm a work in progress, and my life is about progress, not perfection. I tell myself to stop using the words 'always' and 'never' in phrases, like 'I'll always be fat' and 'I'll never be good enough.'" Katie found that small changes such as "eating salads instead of Ding Dongs and saying 'thank you'" were tremendous self-confidence boosters for her.

But what impressed me the most about Katie's baby steps toward creating a new life for herself was how she implemented simple, small changes of self-care. "The one baby step I take every single day is making my bed. It's the one thing I do for myself, so that when I come home at the end of the day I know I took the thirty seconds necessary to provide a nurturing place for myself when I get home. Showing up for life on a daily basis is about those little things you do to take care of yourself in a given twenty-four-hour period, like setting up the coffee the night before. But the one I always remember to do is make my bed."

TAKE A STEP, NO MATTER HOW SMALL

It may be more comfortable for us to sit at home and plan everything out from A to Z before we step out the front door. But by taking one step at a time instead, you'll progress to the next step, and then the next. What's important, and what can be defined as success, is the simple act of taking a step, no matter how small. Take a step in the direction that you feel deeply is the correct path. However tiny, a step in the right direction will help you find yourself on target and on track.

Out of Shape and Overweight

Joe didn't feel he had the confidence to go to a gym. "I'm out of shape and overweight. I'll feel self-conscious about going to the gym. I know that sounds silly, but everyone there is so in shape and I'm huffing and puffing." Nonetheless, Joe defined his vision of being fit and healthy, took an honest assessment of where he was, and made a daily plan for improvement. Joe's plan focused on his ability to take baby steps, and he identified his short-term goal as simply "going to the gym three times a week. It doesn't mean I have to work out so hard I'm soaking wet and burned out, but instead I'll just go and enjoy the time I spend there."

This was a good process for Joe. His vision board included photographs of middle-aged men with big smiles rather than big muscles. He realized that it would be counterproductive and only serve to reinforce his inner critic (who would remind him that he'd been a "Pillsbury Doughboy" as a child) if he compared himself to "buffed-out guys who are twenty years younger than I am. I want to focus on being healthy and enjoying the process," said Joe. So he started small, spending fifteen minutes his first day at the gym, and gradually increased his time by five to ten minutes each visit until he reached two hours. Today, he's lost twenty pounds and is still making daily progress, taking baby steps, and achieving his vision one step at a time.

PRECISE AND SMALL

John Hall, a physician in Australia, studied guided imagery for the development of precise and small surgical skills in physicians. Hall (2002) found that guided imagery was an important tool that helped physicians increase their surgical skills. He found in his investigations that sharpening surgical skill was determined by task definition, prior learning, mental rehearsal and reflection, problem solving, and reality checks. Hall built upon the work of noted scientist Edmund Jacobson, who, in 1931, observed electrical activity within the relevant muscle groups when people were asked to imagine bending their arms or lifting a weight. Consider for a moment how precise and small the electrical activity within a muscle is, yet how large its influence is. Hall understood that Jacobson's findings indicate a neurological mechanism linking the activity in the brain with the body. This also means that guided mental imagery shares the same neural networks of major cognitive functions, such as language, memory, and movement. Hall concluded that there isn't a separate imagery neural network, but rather that all systems are integrally connected. Imagine, then, the precise and small electrical currents running through your body creating major impacts. The infinitesimal molecules that jump from one neuron to another are creating big results.

Awareness Exercise #11

What small changes can you make in your life in pursuit of your chosen confidence goal?

1. In your notebook, start a new page and title it "Small Changes in My Life."

2. Ask yourself the following questions:

   • What small changes can I make in my bedroom, bathroom, wardrobe, and daily routine?

   • What small changes can I make in my life in order to help put me on a path to confidence?

   Small changes can be as simple as purchasing new sheets or a potted plant to brighten your room, buying luxurious bath soaps or a refreshing and fragrant shower gel, sending to Goodwill any ill-fitting, torn, or worn-out clothes, or deciding to see each day as a new opportunity to live fully.

   Making small changes helps to shift your perceptions and awareness of how you live your life. When you shift your perceptions you'll find new options, which will further lead you toward new outcomes and help you develop new levels of confidence. Here are some examples of small changes that other people have used to shift their perspectives in life, open up their awareness, gain insight into living in new ways, and strengthen their confidence in order to create a big impact in their life:

"When I drive home, I take a different route. I'm amazed at what new sights I see and how this opens me up to thinking and acting in new ways."

"When I go to a restaurant, I order something different off the menu. I've discovered food I didn't think I'd like. This is important for me, because now I'm willing to try new things that I wouldn't have before."

"When I go to the market, I don't start at my usual side of the store—I start at the opposite end and go down each aisle in reverse order. I see things I haven't seen before, and taking a different path opens me up to new ideas."

"I like to plant some seeds in a pot on my windowsill. I can watch how the small changes every day eventually bring about a beautiful new flower. It reminds me that even though I don't see what's happening in the soil, something is going on. And I can apply this to my life, knowing that little things do add up to create new results."

"I like to take a big deep breath. Just a simple look out the window or, better yet, a five-minute walk changes my mood dramatically. When my mood shifts, I have more energy to try new things."

"I like to compliment people and see how their eyes light up. It makes me feel good knowing I've made a difference in their life. And when I feel good, I'm not so afraid to try something new myself."

"I put a smile on my face. It lightens me up and makes me feel that I can make a change in my life for the better."

"I like to clean out the closets, have a garage sale, get new sheets, change the oil in my car, or have it tuned up. This makes me feel like I've got things under control and sets into motion all sorts of wonderful new things coming my way."

3. As you consider small changes that you can make in your life, do what seems deeply right at the moment. Ask yourself, "Does this take me closer to my vision, or farther away?" Let yourself explore new ways to increase your level of confidence. Again, when you make new choices, allowing yourself small, incremental baby steps of improvement, you're sending a direct message to your mind and body that you do have what it takes, and that you are moving in the direction of living confidently.

See life as a game to be enjoyed, not as a test to be endured. Life isn't a prison sentence; it's an experience.

Rituals: Meaningful Acts of Behavior

Rituals are very important components in guided imagery practice. Rituals give significance to life's passages, such as birth, weddings, and, of course, death. When rituals are consistent with our beliefs, they have a powerful effect on our attitudes, behavior, self-image, and confidence.

Jeanne Achterberg, a psychologist, along with holistic nurses Barbara Dossey and Leslie Kolkmeier, coauthored the book *Rituals of Healing: Using Imagery for Health and Wellness* (1994), in which they describe rituals as "storage units" of significant amounts of information about a people's beliefs (1994, 4). Rituals honor deep human feelings and our need for sacred connection, and they link the ultimate power of the conscious mind with the imagination.

You may have started to intuitively incorporate rituals into your daily guided imagery practice, such as lighting a candle or taking a sip of cool, refreshing lemon water after your session. These are excellent ways to reinforce your growing self-confidence.

Let's practice a few small personal rituals to banish self-doubt from your life.

Awareness Exercise #12

1. Review your responses to the question in awareness exercise 1 (chapter 1) regarding ways in which self-doubt stops you cold.

2. Write out each of these beliefs associated with self-doubt on a small piece of paper.

3. Next, take the small pieces of paper and bury them, burn them, or put them in your freezer.

In conducting this small ritual, you'll be releasing yourself from the negative imagery and the associated ABCs that have held you captive. When we bury something we place it in the ground for all eternity. When we burn something it is reduced to ashes, which also return to the earth forever. When we place a fear or outdated belief into a freezer, we're removing the emotional heat associated with the belief.

Here's an example of how I performed a small, meaningful ritual.

A FADED PHOTOGRAPH

Returning to my childhood experience of being locked in a freezer, I called to my mind the images and feelings of being locked inside. Placing myself into a safe, relaxed state, like the one you've been experiencing while using your guided imagery scripts, I told myself that I would observe the emotions of the event from a distance, as if I were watching a movie on a screen. The scene in my mind, however, turned out to be in black and white. The images were very crisp with hot whites and dense, heavy blacks. Much like an old black-and-white photograph, the images appeared hard and unyielding.

While holding the image of a black-and-white photograph in my mind, I slowly asked my inner confidence coach, Apollo, to come forward. As Apollo entered my imagination, he brought with him bright morning sunlight, a cool blue sky, and gentle billowy clouds. I asked Apollo to help release me from the confines of the harsh black-and-white freezer. Gently, with his help, I noticed a bright, clear, and crisp morning sun beginning to shine onto the black-and-white photo. Within a few seconds, the harsh photographic image in my mind faded into a monochromatic brown sepia tone, like that of an old photo. This image reminded me of the old faded photographs my mother used to keep on the top shelf of her closet in a shoe box. As I continued to sit with this process for a minute or two, the photo continued to fade even more until it was barely visible.

After I had brought my imagery session to a close, and while sitting with the feelings and sensations that washed over me, I wrote on a small piece of paper, "Trapped in a freezer, backed into a corner and can't get out." I then found an old shoe box, put the piece of paper into the shoe box, and placed it on the highest shelf in my closet. The ritual of putting this shoe box high on my closet shelf was a small change representing how my ABCs of this event were no longer holding any power over me. In going through this ritual, I took the focus off of the actual event in my life and allowed it to fade away.

After a short while, I was then able to take the shoe box down from the closet shelf and bury the small piece of paper. As I placed this small piece of paper in the ground, I asked the earth to take back that which had colored my attitudes, beliefs, behaviors, and thoughts about getting out of tight spaces. I felt at peace and unburdened as a result of this small ritual and immediately the power of the negative imagery was gone. In its place, I could feel the positive images that my inner confidence coach, Apollo, had brought with him: bright morning sunlight, freedom, calmness, and confidence.

RIVER OF THOUGHTS

Below is a wonderful guided imagery script to help you take small steps toward letting go of confidence-sapping negative thoughts. As Jeffrey Brantley, founder and director of Duke University's Mindfulness-Based Stress Reduction Program, and coauthor Wendy Millstine state in their book *Five Good Minutes*, "endless, negative preoccupations and worries steal away our precious energy and leave us drained at the end of the day" (2005, 72)—and they can also deflate our confidence levels.

Use the now-familiar directions for entering a relaxed state of mind and returning to your personal place (see guided imagery exercises 1 through 3 for a reminder). When you are safely there, with your inner confidence coach at your side if you wish, allow yourself to continue with the new script below.

Guided Imagery Exercise #6 ──────────────

1. *Imagine that you are writing all your negative thoughts, worries, and confidence challenges down on little pieces of paper.*

2. *Once you have a sufficient stack, in your mind take a walk to the nearest river.*

    At the river's edge, toss out your harassing thoughts, one by one, saying good-bye to each one.

    Watch the current carry your worries, like delicate leaves, down the river. Notice each nagging thought drift away and out of sight. Use this river to dump out any unwanted anxiety.

3. *When you are finished, you can return to your personal place, and say good-bye to your inner confidence coach.*

4. *After a few moments, begin to bring yourself back to full waking awareness, as you've done in other guided imagery exercises, until you come back to the present, feeling refreshed, unencumbered by unwanted thoughts and anxiety, and more confident.*

The Big Picture

By now you should be getting into the habit of using guided imagery on a regular basis. Each day you're becoming more and more skillful at practicing a variety of self-confident acts in your mind's eye. You are tapping into the power of your imagination and feeling more confident each and every day. The repetition of guided imagery while in a relaxed state of mind is helping you move through barriers with ease. You're expanding your ability to role-play and anticipating several possible responses to many situations. You're becoming clearer and more focused as you recognize that imagery tools can help you overcome self-doubt.

The guided imagery scripts you've been using up until now have the added benefit of lowering your stress levels and lessening daily distractions that sap your self-confidence. Each and every time you practice these imaginary journeys, you'll find yourself becoming more adept at facing new situations in a relaxed state of mind while also strengthening your mental muscles.

By conducting a daily guided imagery practice, regularly reflecting on your vision board, and journaling, you're becoming more vital, courageous, and committed. However, you might feel a bit impatient and wish to begin living up to your full potential immediately. If so, don't worry. View each small change you make as a pebble being dropped into a great ocean. One day soon, you'll see a big impact.

6

trying out new ways of being

"I never hit a shot, not even in practice, without having a
very sharp, in-focus picture of it in my head."
—Jack Nicklaus

Guided imagery is a skill. And like all skills, it needs to be practiced on a daily basis. If you want to develop greater self-confidence to accomplish any goal, you need to be diligent and faithful in
your practice of imagining.

Practice Makes Perfect

Champion golfer Jack Nicklaus knows the power of using guided
imagery for confidence and success. He knows that when practicing

a swing or putt in his mind, it's best to fill the imagery with as much sensory detail as possible. He knows that in order to reach a high level of peak performance he must practice mental repetition of his desired goal. "First, I see the ball where I want it to finish, nice and white and sitting up high on the bright green grass," says Nicklaus. "Then the scene quickly changes, and I see the ball going there: its path, trajectory, and shape, even its behavior on landing. Then there is a sort of fade-out, and the next scene shows me making the kind of swing that will turn the previous images into reality."

Filling in as much detail as possible creates a high-quality image. Think of this kind of mental rehearsal, or "imagery rehearsal," as a test drive. Here you get the chance to try out different scenarios and situations until you're completely at ease with acting in new ways in order to achieve your imagined confidence goal.

THE BENEFITS OF IMAGERY REHEARSAL

Athletes, actors, musicians, and dancers all know that imagery rehearsal allows you to practice what you want to accomplish in the future. During rehearsal you have the opportunity to go through every move, gesture, tone of voice, sight, and smell that will propel you to give an extraordinary performance. Rehearsing in your mind grounds your experience, increases your awareness and perception, helps you get out of your own way, and secures new ABCs of confidence that tell you you have what it takes. Most important, imagery rehearsal helps you to anticipate any and all obstacles that might come up during the actual event you're planning. When you're able to anticipate obstacles or challenges, you can use imagery rehearsal to practice what you would do or say differently. This way, if any surprises come up in the actual event, you've already practiced how you can act so you're not caught off guard. Remember, your brain, mind, and body don't know the difference between an imagined performance and the real thing.

If you've watched Olympic ice skating or gymnasts on television, you've seen the athletes going through their motions backstage, practicing their routines in small steps, sometimes even with their eyes closed. They are anchoring into their body and mind the sensory experience of what they're about to do. Then, when they skate out onto the ice or jump onto the balance beam, their bodies are duplicating and acting out all of the imagery they have mentally rehearsed hundreds of times.

Your peak performance is enhanced by repeated imagery rehearsal when it involves all your senses. It's exactly this mind-body focus that makes guided imagery such a dynamic force in helping us realize our new ways of acting and being. Because you're involving the right hemisphere of your brain, the home of your emotions, you'll also find your self-image, self-esteem, self-efficacy, and self-confidence taking off like a rocket.

In her book *Thriving in Transition: Effective Living in Times of Change*, Marcia Perkins-Reed says that "unless we challenge ourselves [to see] through imagery how our lives could be better, we will tend to make choices that fall within the parameters to which we are accustomed" (1996, 161). Do you really want to get the same results you've always had? Of course not. By practicing your desired achievements in your mind, you will equip yourself with the imagery necessary to attain your desired results. Remember, your new self-knowledge is providing you with new insights and perceptions about yourself, which in turn leads you to realize that you have new options, and those new options lead to new behavior. Through this process, your imagery rehearsal is being reinforced in your mind and body and is boosting your confidence.

But what if you still don't feel confident? Not to worry—you can fake it till you make it.

FAKE IT TILL YOU MAKE IT

If you act as if you're already confident and have what you're seeking, then you're setting up positive beliefs that will result in your success. "Fake it till you make it" means that when you practice new behaviors and new ways of being, you become a magnet for your future achievements. When you practice the body posture, attitudes, beliefs, and behaviors that go along with being confident and self-assured, your body and mind start working together to make it so. Actors, business executives, and athletes all know the value of aligning nonverbal body language and self-image beliefs in order to act as if they already have supreme confidence. One thing is for sure: when you act like a loser, you'll be unsuccessful. When you act like a winner, you'll believe you are a winner and you'll be a winner!

When you "act as if," or "fake it till you make it," you'll notice a difference in your outlook on life. You'll notice yourself walking tall, making eye contact, smiling, and speaking calmly. With enough practice, your self-image will begin to catch up with you, and one day you won't have to pretend. When you "act as if," you're mentally rehearsing your newfound confidence one step at a time. As you practice this, your confidence becomes real and natural and you become grounded in the knowledge that you can do it! And, not only will you persuade yourself that you are confident, but you'll also convey to others that you are confident. When you walk, sit, and talk as if you've got all the self-assurance in the world, people will interpret your behavior as confidence.

Finally, refuse to continue believing and acting small. As Marianne Williamson says in her book *A Return to Love*, "You are a child of God. Your playing small doesn't serve the world" (1996, 191). So be bold. Fake it till you make it, and act as if. Use your imagery rehearsals to practice new behavior and then actually try out new ways of being in your real life. You'll see tremendous changes in your life when you realize that you are a worthy human being.

It's as Easy as Jumping Out of an Airplane

Dan Brodsky-Chenfeld is an internationally recognized champion sky-diver who has won titles at eight World Cup competitions and sixteen National Championships and is the current world-record holder for the largest freefall skydiving formation ever built. When training com-petitive skydivers, Dan incorporates substantial imagery practice in order to help people act in new ways. As he explained to me, "We [sky-divers] have no choice but to use imagery in our training, when you consider that a jump may last only thirty-five to fifty seconds. Because our sessions are so short, we use imagery at least thirty minutes a day, every day, to increase not only our confidence, but our belief that we've got what it takes" (D. Brodsky-Chenfeld, pers. comm.).

Not only does Dan advise constructing and using a formal imagery rehearsal plan, but he also recommends spontaneous practice. Spontaneous practice happens when an image automatically pops into your mind even when you're in the middle of doing something com-pletely unrelated. When Dan finds a skydiving-related image popping into his head, he'll use that image to picture a skydive in vivid detail. In doing so, he's calling on the skill set required to accomplish his goal "anywhere, anytime, even while being distracted by something else." This ensures that Dan's ABCs of confidence (his attitudes, behaviors, and cognitive thought processes) are programmed into his body, mind, and spirit.

When practicing new ways of being, Dan believes it's essential to imagine two different perspectives: one from an observer's position and one from your own. Practicing seeing a situation from multiple points of view will help you imagine yourself in as many variations of that situation as possible. For example, when you use imagery to practice introducing yourself to new people, asking for a raise, interviewing for a new job, or initiating a difficult conversation, use your imagery to rehearse what you will say, how you will dress, and what it will feel like—but also imagine the various ways the other person may see you and respond. Then, when these different scenarios do present themselves to you, you won't be caught off guard or surprised. Why? Because you've already mentally rehearsed various ways of trying out new behavior. You're now ready to achieve your confidence goals!

DEVELOPING AN IMAGERY REHEARSAL PLAN

Jack Jefferies, Dan's teammate and fellow skydiving instructor, has also won multiple world championships and national titles as captain of the U.S. Skydiving Team. Jack knows that "when the ground is rushing up at you at 120 miles per hour, imagery practice is vital to strengthen your belief and behavior, [and that] the use of imagery practice holds true for life as it does for sports." For Jack, "whether I'm doing public speaking or going to a meeting with Mr. Mucky-Muck, an imagery rehearsal plan is imperative." Jack sums up the steps of the rehearsal plan he uses for practicing new ways of behaving:

Repetition: Repeat the same sequence in your mind over and over and over again.

Relaxation: Frequent periods of relaxation between imagery sessions can help you avoid anxiety. When your mind is at ease, you'll think better than when you're uptight and anxious. A relaxed mind is more receptive to learning new things and practicing new behavior than an anxious mind.

Calmness: Producing a calm mind and the proper arousal level is key to practicing new behavior. Use your imagery to practice in an optimal, calm state of mind.

Multiple points of view: View your situation from as many different angles as possible so you can learn to react to changes and surprises as they happen.

Slow motion: Experience your desired goal in slow motion while analyzing all the details.

Double time: Speeding up the motion in your mind to twice the usual speed broadens your anticipation skills and builds confidence.

Real time: Imagining your desired goal or outcome in real time helps your mind practice the sequence, timing, and all the details so they become completely automatic. It's here that you can practice the correct level of arousal, anticipation, distraction control, and all the mental discipline that goes into a great performance.

Positive attitude: Always imagine things working out exactly the way you've planned. You must be careful not to imagine the things you fear! Imagine only what you want to happen.

Process orientation: Imagine executing your desired goal from start to finish, and evaluate your imagery session afterward.

When I asked Jack how he thought imagery rehearsal helped people develop confidence, he told me a personal story. "For years, the U.S. Skydiving Team always came in second place at international competitions. . . . We were always second to the French team and it really got to our confidence. So, we decided to take a different approach. For the next month, each and every day that we were preparing for the next international competition, five days a week, the team started every morning with a thirty-minute guided imagery session. We would mentally rehearse each and every move, and then we decided to add a last section to our rehearsal. We added seeing ourselves standing on the winners' podium, in first place" (J. Jefferies, pers. comm.).

Can you guess what happened to their confidence levels? Any guesses about who won that year's international skydiving competition? That's right. That year, the U.S. Skydiving Team finally scored higher than the French team, and they were proud to stand on the medals podium. Although this book doesn't ask you to jump out of an airplane, you can use the skydivers' imagery rehearsal plan to help you tackle your own confidence challenges. Remember to be intentional every time you imagine, because the power of your mind is strong.

To begin your imagery rehearsal plan, you'll need to first set the scene. Then we'll add lights, costumes, camera, and action!

Setting the Scene

For each situation where you want more confidence, call to mind the exact place you'll be in that scenario. If this is an actual place, such as a hotel conference room where you'll be giving a presentation, you can start by visiting the location and scoping out the room. Fill in all the details as much as you can, including the colors, smells, textures, and sounds, and commit them to memory so you can develop a clear picture of the location in your mind. If this is a place you can't visit beforehand, like an office where you'll be interviewing for a job, focus your attention on your feelings of unshakeable confidence so that, whatever the situation or location, you know you're prepared to handle anything that comes your way.

Lights, Costumes, Camera, and Action

How you dress can have an amazing impact on your confidence levels. If you've ever heard the phrase "The clothes make the man," then you know that how you're dressed can add or detract from your confidence.

Jan was in a midcareer transition, having just opened her own consulting business, which she ran from her home. She felt that she lacked the confidence to make the cold calls or follow-up phone calls that would help to increase her client list. As we talked, she described the setting in her kitchen where she made her calls and how she introduced herself and her business to prospective clients. One of the things she liked about working from home was that she didn't have to get dressed up each and every day in heels and makeup. But, she explained, when she was trying to muster her confidence to make calls she was often dressed in her bathrobe and fuzzy slippers, with her hair still in curlers. Not a good recipe for success!

What Jan hadn't realized was that she hadn't set the proper scene, nor was she in costume and ready for action. Without these key elements, all of her imagery rehearsals went down the drain. I suggested to Jan that on those days when she needed to make business telephone calls, she put on her professional clothes and makeup, and that, instead of sitting down by the telephone, she stand up while speaking. When she did this, she was in a professional frame of mind; she was in costume and ready for her close-up! A month later Jan called to tell me that the simple action of getting dressed and standing up made her sound and act more confident. As a result, her business was taking off and new clients were coming to her from referrals.

Practicing New Ways of Behaving

Now let's bring your imagery rehearsal to life. Focus your concentration and attention on your confidence goal. Stay present and let go of thoughts or images of failure, self-doubt, or rejection. Breathe slowly and remember your personal place. Bring in your symbol of confidence, and invite your inner confidence coach to join you. Now imagine yourself in the situation you want to feel confident about: you're sure of yourself, steady, and ready. Your imagery plan will help you manage and control your feelings of anxiety and will help you stay motivated.

Remember, what you focus on becomes magnified. So don't focus on past mistakes or past failures. The past is over and you now have the power to replace all the negative images in your mind with new positive ones. Thomas Edison spent years trying to create a lightbulb. But he once told a colleague, "I have not failed; I've discovered twelve hundred materials that don't work." Reframe your experience, choose your words carefully, and focus on the positive. If your goal is to increase your confidence and stick to your exercise routine, you might focus on the positive by imagining how good it will feel to fit into that pair of pants you've been saving. Can you hear the sound of the zipper easily closing? Imagine what others might say to you: "Wow—you look great! You did it! Congratulations! You're a winner!"

Below, you'll find several imagery rehearsals useful for various scenarios, and suggestions for setting the scene and adding lights, camera, costumes, and action. Find the script that is closest to your personal situation and mentally rehearse it. Then, working with a trusted friend or by yourself, actually practice new ways of being.

Meeting New People at a Party

Imagine walking confidently into a party and introducing yourself to new people. In your mind's eye, rehearse this scene over and over, with all sorts of different scenarios. Before you start, tell yourself, "I can do it!"

What are you wearing?

What sounds do you hear, such as voices or music?

What time of day or night is it?

Can you smell food cooking?

Imagine walking up to someone and saying, "Hi, my name is _____."

Imagine having a pleasant conversation full of smiles and laughter.

Remember to relax; confident people don't walk into a party tense and uptight.

Imagine talking to someone; say the words out loud, and hear yourself speaking calmly.

Imagine this scenario in slow motion. What details can you sense?

Fast-forward through your conversation. Make it end the way you want it to end. You're in control of what you create in your imagery.

Now, take what you've learned from your imagery rehearsal plan and practice it. You can do this in the privacy of your own home, perhaps in front of your bathroom mirror, or in the kitchen—someplace where you feel comfortable. Get dressed in the clothes you imagine yourself wearing. You might even want to buy a new blouse or shirt so you feel really great. Practice your introduction; hear yourself actually saying the words that you imagined during your rehearsal. Say the words out loud. Remember to breathe and speak slowly and calmly.

Asking Someone for a Date

Imagine that you're at a party and you want to ask someone out for a date. Or imagine yourself standing by the phone, ready to make that all-important phone call. Below are several possible scenarios that you can mentally rehearse.

First, assess your emotions and how your body is feeling. If you feel tense and uptight, then you may also feel hot. Imagine that your hands are in a bucket of ice cubes. The cool ice will calm the raging fire in your mind.

If you're anxious, you may find yourself feeling cold. If so, imagine you're lying in the grass on a warm summer day and the sunlight is baking your body.

If you're scared, you might imagine you are wrapped up in a soft, smooth deep-green comforter, soothing your heart and mind.

As you pick up the phone to make the call, or as you stand before the person you'd like to ask out, remember that you are enough. Imagine saying the words you will use. Say the words out loud and hear the right level of confidence in your voice.

Imagine a wonderful, fun-filled date, with good food, pleasant conversation, and the feeling that you are confident.

Imagine hearing the words "Yes, I'd love to go out with you!"

Consider practicing with a friend who will give you honest feedback. With this trusted friend, and your imagery rehearsal firmly planted in your mind, say out loud the words you'll use to ask the person out. They could be as simple as "I'd really like to have dinner with you so we can become better acquainted." Ask your friend for feedback. Are you coming on too strong or too weak? Does your body language contradict your words? Are you speaking too fast or too slow? As you act out the scene, practicing the words and body language you'll eventually be using, remember to keep in your mind a clear vision of confidence, peace, calmness, and serenity. No one wants to date someone who seems anxious.

Going on a Job Interview

Going on a job interview can be nerve-wracking, to say the least. After all, you're not usually given the chance to reinterview for a job if at first you don't succeed. And there are a lot of unknowns: you may not know much about the people you could eventually be working with, and in the interview you might be meeting with just a senior executive or even a committee of strangers. You might feel shy about discussing your strengths or selling yourself. As in skydiving, you may not get much practice at interviewing for a specific job. To lessen any anxiety, you can use the same approach to rehearse in your mind exactly how you want the interview to proceed.

Imagine hitting a home run, hearing the crowd roar its approval, and feeling the exhilaration of the moment.

Hear the sound of a cork popping out of a champagne bottle to celebrate your new job.

Imagine that the people you are interviewing with are genuinely interested in you and see that you could be a perfect match.

Feel your inner confidence coach standing by your shoulder giving you constant encouragement as the interview progresses.

Interviewing for a new job does take practice. With the imagery rehearsal techniques above firmly planted in your mind, you can practice by going on informational interviews, which allow you to collect new information and hone your interview skills. You can ask questions without the pressure of wondering whether you'll get the job. Remember Joan, who created a smaller version of her vision board in her notebook and took it with her on job interviews? By keeping her mind focused on her vision, and practicing with imagery rehearsal, she was able to concentrate on matching her vision to her future job.

Public Speaking

Even experienced public speakers frequently feel nervous, but they don't let their nerves get the better of them. Many veteran actors even utilize their stage fright to keep on their toes. Effective speakers look and act confident, making eye contact, moving with ease, and using humor to take the edge off. Imagery rehearsal and actual practice can help you become a confident public speaker. If there are opportunities for you to practice public speaking while at work you may want to volunteer for these assignments. Here are some practical tips for rehearsing public speaking.

Imagine hearing the sound of applause.

See yourself standing confidently at the podium.

Imagine yourself easily answering any and all questions that come your way.

Picture yourself being so familiar with your talk that you don't need to look at your notes.

See your presentation running smoothly.

Visualize the smiling faces in the crowd nodding their heads in agreement.

Asking for a Raise

Let's say you want to ask your boss for a raise. As you learned in the previous chapters, the relationship between confidence and fear is pretty close. You might imagine your boss barking at you, "Are you crazy? At a time like this?" Nonetheless, you can rehearse in your mind what you want to say and your reasons for deserving a raise, and use imagery to decrease your fears. Imagine your boss's office in great detail. Can you sense the time of day? Asking for a raise is about believing in your own natural state of abundance. Here are a few imagery tips to contemplate.

> Imagine that you're standing on a wonderful mountain with your arms outstretched, taking in all the wonders and abundance of the world.

> See yourself walking along the seashore, with gentle waves lapping at your feet, sensing abundance in all aspects of your life. Like the endless sea, the world holds plenty of riches for you.

> Envision a movie playing on a television screen in your mind, a movie that depicts lack and scarcity. Now, in your imagination, pick up the remote control and gradually turn down the volume, so you're not hearing the negative words about scarcity. Then flip the channel to show a different movie, one in which you're achieving your dreams of confidence.

Dealing with Self-Consciousness

Self-doubt is often accompanied by self-consciousness and shyness. You might be focusing too intensely on your perceived shortcomings. If you walk into a party and feel overcome with self-consciousness, shift your focus away from yourself. Instead of ruminating on what you're going to say, trust that the right words will come to you. Ask your inner confidence coach to stand next to you and help you keep the conversation going. Self-confident people rarely focus on themselves.

Imagine a magic wand touching your forehead and giving you all the power and confidence you seek.

Imagine having the qualities of strength, wisdom, integrity, courage, and faith. Do not listen to the feelings of fear, doubt, insecurity, self-consciousness, or guilt. Banish them to a deserted tropical island, or change the channel on your mental television.

Picture yourself throwing a bucket of water onto the Wicked Witch, or clobbering the Ogre of Self-Doubt.

See your inner confidence coach, your guardian angel, or a beloved relative watching out for you.

Envision a candle burning brightly and strong, signifying your personal light shining forth.

Begin to see any feelings of self-consciousness or shyness as an asset and strength. In her book *The Highly Sensitive Person* (1997), psychotherapist Elaine Aron writes that your heightened self-awareness is a trait that is valuable in our society. Being sensitive is all in how you look at it, and how you frame your self-image. Your sensitivity is really a remarkable ability to pick up on subtle clues, with insight, empathy, and creativity. Your imagery rehearsal can help you prepare for times when you're overstimulated, and it can help keep you calm so you can act according to your own personal style of confidence.

GENERAL SELF-CONFIDENCE IMAGERY REHEARSALS

Below are a number of general self-confidence imagery rehearsal plans that you can undertake anytime or anywhere. You may find it useful to add these to the end of your daily relaxation practice, to help you overcome any feelings of self-doubt. Imagine the following sensory experiences and scenarios:

You're sipping ice-cold champagne and hearing a toast of "Congratulations!"

You're walking down the aisle at your wedding.

Your vision board is communicating to you specific actions and behaviors you can take. You can hear and sense with your full body all the messages that come to you intuitively.

You're in a protective transparent bubble that keeps you free from harm. All your good intentions can pass through the bubble's exterior easily and effortlessly, but the negative energy of others cannot pass through this protective layer.

You're standing on top of the world.

You're at a wonderful mountain retreat, your own private Shangri-la.

You're floating above the Earth in a special spaceship or riding on a magic carpet, high above the ground. Can you see how small your problems now look?

You're being assisted and supported by Mother Teresa or another figure of great serenity and assurance, such as Jesus, Buddha, Muhammad, Moses, or Confucius.

Commit to these confidence-building imagery rehearsals. Be willing to be open, imagine the scene vividly in your mind, and fake it 'til you make it. Now it's time to utilize a guided imagery exercise to help strengthen your own supreme confidence.

Your Ideal Self

Your ideal self is a compilation of healthy self-esteem, positive self-image, and strong self-efficacy, all rolled up into one. Return to the opening sections of the guided imagery script that you've been using to enter a state of deep relaxation and visit your personal place. The more you use this script, the more you'll condition your mind and body to easily and effortlessly enter a state of deep peace. You'll find with just a few simple breaths that you're safe and secure. When you feel that your body is relaxed, follow the remainder of this script.

Guided Imagery Exercise #7

1. *Allow an image of yourself to form in your mind. See yourself exactly as you'd like to be—just the way you want to see yourself when you envision your future. What are you wearing? Where are you? Who else is around you?*

2. *Notice how good it feels to be confident, assured, and able to speak your truth.*

3. *Pay attention to the most noticeable qualities and strengths of your ideal self.*

4. *Choose an event that you'd like to prepare for in the future. Invite your confidence coach to join you. You could be going to a party, asking someone for a date, or interviewing for a new job. As you project yourself into the future, imagine the setting in as much detail as you can. What time of day is it? What are you doing? In your mind, break down your behaviors into tiny baby steps, noticing each sequential step deeply and profoundly. Spend a few moments here and imagine supreme confidence. Your inner confidence coach is standing right next to you, saying, "You are doing a great job. You can be proud of yourself."*

5. *Next, imagine that you are repeating new behavior that supports your ever-growing confidence. In particular, imagine yourself relaxed, calm, and self-assured.*

6. *In your mind, speed up the motion of your behavior, or let it slow down so you can observe each and every detail.*

7. *Perhaps you can see yourself from various viewpoints. In your mind, you can be the actor and the director, viewing yourself as you would through a camera, from above, below, the side, far away, and up close.*

8. *When you feel that you have rehearsed each and every step, you can say good-bye to these images and sensations, knowing you can return to this time and place any time you want, simply by calling forth the feelings and emotions of being fully confident.*

9. *Take a few slow, energizing breaths, and wiggle your toes and fingers as you begin to come back to full awareness. Know that everything in your life is unfolding exactly as it should, and that you are always doing your very best. When you are ready, open your eyes, feeling refreshed, confident, calm, and at peace.*

10. *When you have returned to full waking consciousness, remember to write down in your notebook all the feelings, images, ideas, and thoughts that came to you during your session.*

The Big Picture

You are capable of living your dreams. When you pursue your visions and goals, act as if you have already attained the supreme confidence you're seeking and fake it 'til you make it. Walk tall, carry your head high, make eye contact, and speak deliberately. The right words will come to you. Make a habit of practicing exactly how you want to perform. The real risk is in not pursuing your dreams. Remember, you can always go back to the safe and comfortable choices you've made in the past. But is that really what you want to do?

Working with imagery is a skill, and as with any skill you'll need to practice it in order to accomplish your goals. Success in using guided imagery for self-confidence depends on developing and following an imagery rehearsal plan. Developing self-confidence also depends on focusing on what's right. Let's now look at what's right with you, just as you are at this very moment in time.

7

focusing on what's right

"Ordinary riches can be stolen, real riches cannot.
In your soul are infinitely precious things that cannot
be taken from you." —Oscar Wilde

It's human nature to compare ourselves to others. We want to know
how we stack up against our next-door neighbor, peers, or coworkers. But it's important to remember that when you constantly compare
yourself to others—especially when you want to act in new and confident ways—you're engaging in a losing battle. Using guided imagery
on a regular basis will help you keep the focus on your uniqueness,
your individual "golden nuggets of strength."

Golden Nuggets of Strength

When you're faced with situations that challenge your self-confidence, you may automatically see your glass as half empty. When you believe your glass is half empty, you may find yourself in a self-limiting mindset, putting yourself down with a chorus of "I can't." You convince yourself that you don't have what it takes. Your inner critic scampers around tripping you up, reinforcing negative ABCs, and ensuring that you have a negative self-image. When this happens, anger, worry, frustration, fear, and self-doubt become knee-jerk reactions, just like a bad habit.

But you've learned by now that these reactions don't reflect the truth. Bad-habit knee-jerk reactions are just that—habitual reactions based upon past lies. These reactions are automatic feedback that comes from years of focusing on negative untruths rather than positive truths. But now you have a way of countering that negative feedback and getting yourself back on track. In this book, you've learned that you can call upon your inner confidence coach any time and any place to remind you that you are strong, capable, and worthy. You've learned how to bring forth mind-based skills to overcome self-defeating attitudes, and how to use imagery rehearsal to imagine and then create a new life. The skills you've learned have been training you to focus on what's right with you, instead of what's wrong. In fact, this book up until now has been geared toward helping you live a life of confidence and ease, shifting your perspective so you can see the riches that make up your signature strengths—strengths that are uniquely yours. All you have to do is tell yourself, "I can do it! I do have what it takes!" Shift your perspective, reframe your experience, and use imagery to focus on what's right, good, and positive.

SHIFT YOUR PERSPECTIVE TO THE POSITIVE

Confidence is built upon your signature strengths, not upon your weaknesses. Simply by changing your perspective to view the positive and not focusing on the negative, you will find that your ABCs of confidence fall right into place. When you believe you can do it, you can achieve your confidence goals.

It's human nature, however, to discount the golden nuggets that make up the riches of our personality since we're so used to them, or because we take them for granted. Countless times I've heard people say, "Well, doesn't everyone have these same strengths?" The answer, clearly, is no. Your strengths are individual and distinct, belonging to you alone. Your strengths and individuality are as unique as your fingerprints. No two are alike, and it's these unique golden nuggets, or strengths, that represent the glorious riches of you—riches that can never be taken away from you.

It's understandable that until now you may have focused more intently on what you can't accomplish than on what you can. Every day, all sorts of negative reinforcements swirl around us, such as in the ever-present advertising images that depict the perfect woman or the perfect man. But you must realize that these idealized images are specifically designed to make you believe that you need this toothpaste or that dress to be really confident.

The very nature of psychology itself has even focused on the negative, with its concentration on excavating the problem areas in patients' lives. But now, the profession of psychology is moving toward focusing on what's right, positive, and optimistic in the world. Let's understand this shift as it applies to your confidence and look at why professional psychology is now beginning to focus on the positive instead of the negative. In doing so, you'll better understand how you can shift your own perspective to all of your unique strengths and the positive.

POSITIVE PSYCHOLOGY

For decades the professional practice of psychology was narrowly focused on pathology and mental illness. Although we've learned a lot about hurts, depression, anxiety, and the biological causes of true mental illness, more and more people have begun to ask, "How can I live a better life? What can I do for myself to bring more confidence, happiness, and fulfillment to my life?" Positive-oriented psychology concentrates on answering these questions by channeling signature strengths, assets, skills, and talents for optimal performance. And guided imagery is an integral part of professional psychology's shift from illness to wellness, empowering you to discover or rediscover your active role in creating solutions in your life.

The term "positive psychology" initially grew out of the work of psychologists Abraham Maslow and Carl Rogers, who founded humanistic psychology in the 1950s. Humanistic psychology emerged as a reaction to the two traditional schools of thought that had been popular up until this time. The first school of thought, now called the "first force" of psychology, was behaviorism. Behaviorism, focusing on human behavior as a response to a stimulus, grew out of Ivan Pavlov's work on classical conditioning (remember hearing about dogs salivating in response to the sound of a bell that told them food was on the way?) and was further developed by B. F. Skinner. The other school of thought was Freud's psychoanalysis, commonly referred to as the "second force" of psychology, which focused on repressed emotions and unresolved childhood issues. Humanistic psychology, which eventually became known as the "third force" of psychology, was developed with the belief that professional psychology should focus on the development of the individual self: self-esteem, health, creativity, spirituality, meaning, and actual human emotions and experiences such as love, beauty, and hope (Aanstoos, Serlin, and Greening 2000). Today, the aim of humanistic psychology is to support a holistic view of each person, and, as you've learned, this holistic mind-and-body perspective is also a crucial element of success with guided imagery.

Humanistic Psychology and Optimism

Humanistic psychology tends to take a predominantly positive outlook on life and human beings. Over the years, many people have worked to refine the concepts of positive psychology. Martin Seligman and Mihaly Csikszentmihalyi, working together and independently, both describe how life-changing it can be to shift away from a mental-illness perspective and emphasize what people do well (Seligman 1998, 2002; Seligman and Csikszentmihalyi 2000; Csikszentmihalyi 1997, 2001). Seligman describes the elements that make up a good, meaningful, and full life as well-being, creativity, courage, kindness, generosity, and experiencing and savoring both positive emotions (such as happiness, fun, relaxation, and authenticity) and positive sensory feelings (tastes, smells, sight, sounds, and body movement) derived from your signature strengths.

Your task in life is to deploy your signature strengths and virtues in the major realms of life: work, love, parenting, and finding and living a purposeful and meaningful existence. This is where guided imagery plays an important role. Guided imagery rehearsal actually shifts the focus from the things you can't do to those you can do. By shifting your perspective to the positive and being optimistic, with the guidance and support of your inner confidence coach, vision board, and imagery rehearsal, you can find a deeper purpose as you begin to reclaim yourself and live with confidence.

The aim of positive or optimistic psychology therefore is to enable you to live a life filled with greater health, well-being, and meaning. Let's identify some of the strengths that are a part of you and see how they connect to the ABCs of confidence and guided imagery.

YOU CAN DO IT!

Guided imagery makes use of all the elements of positive psychology and is a natural complement to your efforts to build upon your strengths, skills, and talents. When you use imagery rehearsal for confidence, you're able to encourage and build upon what's right with you and the golden nuggets that are your strengths. When you focus on your belief that you are powerful, you'll banish negativity and find that you do have what it takes to turn your positive imagery into reality.

What are your signature strengths? You don't know? Well, could they be enthusiasm, leadership, creativity, originality, humor, persistence, curiosity, and kindness? Whatever they are, your strengths are an authentic part of you at a very deep level, and they confirm that you are enough. The next section will help you identify your signature strengths.

Uncovering Your Signature Strengths

Carlene and Carolyn DeRoo, mother-and-daughter coauthors of *What's Right with Me*, state that "you must have a means of reminding yourself of all the reasons why you are good, worthy, wonderful, talented, beautiful, and unique" (2006, 7). When you focus on what's right instead of what's wrong, your ability to enjoy life increases, and you have more control of your destiny. Your confidence soars and you find yourself stronger, happier, and healthier.

Feeling good about yourself also reduces feelings of insecurity. Focusing on your strengths, you'll find that you don't need to lash out at others to mimic the feeling of confidence. Instead, secure in your worthiness and inherent value as a human being, you are able to make yourself available to others, achieve higher goals, and accept that you are enough. Indeed, for Carlene and Carolyn DeRoo, "living with great self-confidence is a service to others" (2006, 17).

When you let go of the old negative images in your mind and shift your perspective to the positive, you open your eyes to being fully empowered. You're living consistently with the advice that Marianne Williamson gives us when she states, "you were born to make manifest the glory of God that is within us" (1996, 191). And who are you not to fully embrace the strengths and talents that have been bestowed upon you? Your strengths are there to be enjoyed, expressed, and developed. So, even though you may still feel a little uncomfortable patting yourself on the back, you can do it. It's almost like you're growing new skin.

Awareness Exercise #13

The following awareness exercise by Carlene and Carolyn DeRoo, reprinted here with permission, will help you identify your signature strengths, discover what's right with you, and remember how great you actually are. Start a new page in your journal and answer each of the questions below. Feel free to write as much as you want in response to each question, and remember that there are no right or wrong answers. Just write what you feel.

1. What two things do you secretly believe you are good at but never tell anyone? Are you a great kisser, for instance? Good at math, or driving around curves?

2. What have you invested time in exploring? Nutrition? Sailing? Civil War history? Spirituality?

3. For what have you worked very hard?

4. What aspects of you do others appreciate? Do people often tell you that you have a good sense of humor? Are people amazed at your patience?

5. Think of a time when you said yes to something that you wanted, even if it meant some sacrifice or complication.

6. Write down one physical activity that you are good at. You can call yourself a good swimmer even if you haven't been in a pool in years.

7. Recall a creative capability. Do you make crafts, cultivate a garden, paint, or raise children?

8. Record a social skill that you possess. Are you good at staying in touch with friends or putting people at ease?

9. Which self-care activities do you do? Do you exercise regularly? Do you get therapy when you need it?

10. Think of a risk that paid off.

11. Write about one "bad habit" you have that someone else has appreciated. This should be something that is not injurious to you or others. Do others giggle when you barge into rooms and then ask if it's okay to come in?

12. Look back on a compassionate act or a moment of understanding toward yourself or another. What did you do? What enabled you to do it?

13. When have you surprised yourself with your own courage?

GROWING NEW SKIN

Becoming comfortable with your strengths and new levels of optimism can make you a bit uneasy at first. Like a snake crawling out of its old skin, you are now shedding old beliefs, old attitudes, and old behaviors. And like the snake, which needs to sit in the sun for a while and dry its tender new skin, you may need some time to get accustomed to the new you, thinking and acting as a confident person. Here's an easy way to become more comfortable with your strengths.

Awareness Exercise #14

1. Find a favorite old photograph of yourself, one that shows you smiling or enjoying a special moment in life—perhaps a photograph from your wedding or graduation, or a really great vacation. Look for a photograph of you at a time when you felt on top of the world, appreciated, and con-

fident. Now, take this photograph and paste it onto the center of your vision board. Stand back and look at your vision board with you in the center, and remember how good it felt to be this happy and positive. Now, take a few moments to answer the following questions in your notebook about the photograph you've selected:

What were you doing?

Where were you?

Who else was with you?

How were you dressed?

How did it feel to be happy and positive?

2. As you look back over your responses to these questions, see if you note any similarities between your answers in awareness exercise 13. Are you celebrated or appreciated by others for your strengths? Did you accomplish a big risk, like finishing a college degree or getting a promotion? Does the photograph show you in some sort of creative endeavor, or in a situation where you surprised yourself with your courage and conviction? Whatever your response, keep the image of your smiling face foremost in your mind. Firmly plant it in your consciousness and tell yourself you can remember the feeling of being positive, happy, and optimistic any time you wish. When you remember happy times, you're solidifying your beliefs that you are living a confident and successful life. With this acceptance of your life as it is, you're embracing your signature strengths and authoring your own authentic life.

Authenticity, Autonomy, and Authorship

You—not your parents, family, friends, children, or society—are the author of your own life. You are the one who has the power and the resources to author your own life story. No one can ever take away your right to choose your life as you want it to be, nor can they ever take away your genuine signature strengths. These signature strengths mirror your authenticity, autonomy, and authorship. The root of all three of these words comes from the Greek *autos*, meaning "the individual self, directed from within"—in short, meaning "coming from within you."

AUTHENTICITY

Over four hundred years ago, Shakespeare gave us an elemental truth about living authentically when he wrote in *Hamlet*, "This above all: to thine own self be true" (Shakespeare 1980, 1080). To be authentic is to be genuine and follow your true north, your own internal compass, to find what is right and good for you. When you live life from an authentic place that is solidly based on your signature strengths, people respect you for speaking your truth. Remember, no one can make you feel less than authentic unless you give them power to do so. And that, my friend, is something you don't need to do anymore.

AUTONOMY

The word "autonomy" is also built on the Greek word *autos,* paired with the root word *nomos*, meaning "law." Autonomy is the ability to determine one's internal law, or freedom from external authority. Being true to yourself means that you take your own counsel, assisted by your board of directors, your inner confidence coach, and your vision of confidence. It isn't selfish to take care of yourself and to depend on your own opinions. Certainly, you can ask others for their insight, but the ultimate authority in your life is you.

AUTHORSHIP

An "author" is described as a master, or one who brings something about—an inventor, a creator, with the right and power to command. You are the creator of your life story, and you have the power to choose how you'll react to situations and circumstances around you. You have the ability to choose what imagery and thoughts to focus on. You have the imagination to free yourself from false evidence masquerading as protection or support. When you reflect on your vision board, remember that you were the one who created this worthwhile vision of your future success and confidence. You, with all your abundance, have the power to create your world the way you want it to be.

Abundance and Your Self-Confidence

We tend to think of "abundance" as a term that describes material possessions, money, or fame. Yet, in actuality, it is your very personality that makes you abundant, in the truest sense of the word. You were born into a natural state of abundance: an overflowing, full, ample supply of signature strengths, passion, creativity, and love—in short, the things that make you yourself. When you consider it from this perspective, your golden nuggets of authenticity are abundantly manifest in you.

One way to express your natural abundance is to look at what makes you feel luxurious. Music, a good dinner, gourmet ice cream, a manicure, a vase of fresh flowers, bath gels, new socks, new tires, a pretty postcard that you send to yourself—they can all reflect back to you the reasons you're glad to be alive. When you do things that make you feel good about yourself or about others, you're radiating the golden qualities of your mind, body, and spirit.

More important, when you allow yourself to enjoy good things in life, you're sending an unmistakable message to your mind that you are worthy: you're worth having supreme confidence in life, you're worth being successful, and above all else you are worthy of having the life you dream of. When you shift your perspective so that you can enjoy the things in life that make you feel worthwhile, you're focusing on the true nature of prosperity, the spiritual principle that supports your natural birthright. Chi, your vital life force energy, flows in and around you; abundance, optimism, healthy self-esteem, and self-confidence are yours. Remember: whatever you focus on magnifies. So focus on yourself in a positive manner, and your positive view of yourself will be magnified.

Kathy came to my university coaching class wanting to feel more confident in her search for a new job. She had stayed stuck in a job that no longer fit her personality, yet she felt she didn't have what she needed even to begin a new job search. I asked Kathy to do three small self-pampering things for herself over the course of the next week, things that made her feel good. The following week she told me about an out-of-town wedding she had attended. All the guests had stayed at a nice hotel for the weekend, and Kathy had found herself in a luxurious suite, filled with oversized bath towels, a fresh fruit basket, and other soothing amenities. "However, when I put on the fluffy bathrobe, I didn't feel like I deserved to wear it," said Kathy. "It felt too good for me, and I longed for my old torn and tattered bathrobe. I definitely didn't feel like I was worthy of a nice bathrobe." Now, at first glance this might seem silly to focus on, but as Kathy and I discussed the situation in greater detail she came to realize that her tattered old bathrobe summed up her feelings of low self-worth and self-esteem. She came to a new understanding of how her lack of confidence stemmed from her feelings that she was not worthy of the best life has to offer.

With this new self-realization, Kathy said, "It was like a lightbulb suddenly lit up in my head. I am worthy of confidence, success, and all the good things in life! I do deserve to wear a nice bathrobe!" Not so surprisingly, Kathy soon bought a new bathrobe for herself, and later she told me that this simple, small change, full of deeper meaning and significance, was the key to her moving forward with interviewing for a new job. Two months later, Kathy found the job of her dreams and said, "I never would have imagined that something as simple as being good to myself would have such a dramatic impact."

In order to reaffirm your sense of natural abundance and innate worthiness, try out the two exercises below. The first is an awareness exercise. After you have finished it, follow it as soon as you can with the subsequent guided imagery exercise. When you've finished both, return to your notebook and answer the question "What makes me feel worthy of confidence?"

Awareness Exercise #15

1. Over the course of the next week, spend one hour in a quiet, natural outdoor setting. Leave your iPod or Walkman at home, turn off your cell phone, and enjoy the silence. You can walk along the seashore, climb a mountain, take a long walk in a meadow, soak your feet in a babbling brook, or sit under a tree. Whatever you choose to do, feel the essence of nature all around you. Literally stop and smell the roses, as well as the clean air, pine needles, green grass, or ocean breeze. Open your senses to feel the sun on your face, hear the birds singing, and get in touch with the abundance of the world that is all around you.

2. When you have completed your hour, make sure to jot down in your notebook what images and thoughts came into your mind. Make a note of how relaxed you feel and how your breathing has returned to a slow and peaceful rhythm.

Guided Imagery Exercise #8

Allow yourself to imagine the following scenes:

You're floating in an Olympic-size pool of milk and honey. The sweet smell of honey relaxes you while the milk soothes your body.

You're standing under a gentle tropical waterfall, where the clean mountain water is rinsing away all fears and doubts.

You're standing on top of a beautiful mountain, perhaps like the one shown in the opening scene of The Sound of Music. *You can see the green grass and blue sky. Imagine in front of you a freestanding white door. Walk up to the door, and open it. Step through this magic portal to the other side of life, feeling strong, confident, and poised.*

You've found a secret chamber full of precious gems and stones.

You've found a sack of money on a sidewalk. As you open the sack, you see that it has one million dollars inside.

You've won the lottery.

You're wrapping yourself in a luxurious, soft cashmere bathrobe in the color of your preference. This is a special bathrobe that will heal all your past wounds and hurts, take away all stress and worry, and allow you to return to your natural state of abundance and confidence.

Celebrating and Pampering Yourself with Abundance

Confident people know that self-care is critical to their self-esteem and well-being. They know that it's okay to relax as a means of celebrating their strengths and talents and unwinding from the daily stresses of life. Pampering yourself means you know that you deserve good, healthy, positive growth in your life. It means that you are renewing your self-image, which will result in heightened levels of self-confidence. You're not being selfish—you're taking care of yourself—and there's a big difference between the two.

To support a sense of abundance in your life, create your own home spa to celebrate yourself. Like guided imagery, a home spa will help you get in touch with all your senses, revitalize your body, and lower your stress level. And using guided imagery you'll be able to immediately call back to your mind, whenever you're feeling stressed, the pleasant healing experience of enjoying your home spa. When you take care of yourself, you'll polish the golden nuggets that are your signature strengths and revitalize your outlook on life, which will in turn increase your self-confidence.

SENSORY ELEMENTS FOR YOUR HOME SPA

First, you'll want to set aside a space in your home for your personal spa—a place that is soothing and comforting. Below you'll find suggestions for creating a space that stimulates all of your senses and calms your nerves.

Sight

Use colors liberally in your home spa to soothe your mind or energize your body. Pastels such as light blue for water and sky, green for earth, and warm hues that match your skin tone will make you feel at home. The color red will stimulate your passion and boost your vitality, orange will stimulate your creativity and productivity, while yellow will increase your sense of personal power and alertness. Colors can add balance and harmony to your world and refer to different sensations and emotional states.

Touch

Self-massage is an excellent way to relax your body. Massage your neck, shoulders, lower back, hands, and feet.

What does confidence feel like to you? A soft cashmere sweater? Silk? The freshness of new socks, or a new scarf? Surround yourself with things that convey confidence to you.

Sound

Listening to your favorite music can calm you down or pump you up, making you feel optimistic. Music can also have a cleansing and revitalizing effect on your body and mind. What music makes you want to get up and dance? What tunes lull you to sleep? Choose music that celebrates you, and play it on your home stereo or load it onto your personal music player. You might even pick one piece of music that makes you feel strong and confident. Then, whenever you need a little boost, you can listen to this music in your car, at the gym, or anywhere.

Smell

What smells evoke good memories of confident times for you? You can use aromatherapy to relax, unwind, and calm your mind and body, and also to increase your energy. Choose some of the following essential oils or flower essences (available at many health food stores) to renew your confidence. You can use them as bath oils, heat them up in a special holder to release their fragrances into the air, or use incense to bring their aromas to your home spa. You can also rub a small drop of oil on your wrists, on the back of your neck, or in the middle of your forehead.

- Lavender soothes your mind and body when you're feeling stressed and under pressure, and it can also be used to treat insomnia. Add four to six drops to your bathwater or sprinkle some on the shower floor before stepping inside (taking care not to slip).

- Chamomile heals any irritability and promotes good sleep.

- Rose helps relieve overworked emotions, lifts your spirits, and provides just the right soothing aroma for peace and happiness.

- Sandalwood incense or essential oil encourages relaxation.

- Geranium can calm your body and soul and relieve anxiety and stress.

- Ginger, gently massaged on the skin over your kidneys, will revive your energy.

- Lemon will boost your spirits and strengthen your immune system.

- Rosemary will raise your energy level and leave you feeling supercharged and ready to face the day.

- Juniper will eliminate toxins from your body and leave you feeling refreshed, calm, and confident.

One word of caution: if you are pregnant or nursing, consult with your medical professional before using any essential oils or flower remedies.

Taste

Bach flower remedies, developed by physician Edward Bach (1886–1936), are distilled liquids from plants and flowers for homeopathic treatments. Each of the thirty-eight remedies discovered by Dr. Bach is directed at a particular characteristic or emotional state. You can purchase small bottles at most health food stores. You might consider trying the following Bach flower remedies:

- Larch is intended to heal self-doubt and helps people who do not consider themselves as good or capable as others around them.

- Elm may be used when you are feeling overwhelmed by responsibility.

- Aspen is formulated to alleviate fear of unknown things in life.

Remember that healthy foods play a large part in helping you feel in balance and able to cope with stress. Keep a supply of healthy snacks available all day long, and try eating smaller meals more frequently throughout the day. Here are a few examples of healing and balancing foods to try, in concert with your home spa activities:

- Bananas are rich in potassium, zinc, and iron and help to soothe the digestive system.

- Celery is a cleansing and anti-inflammatory food that helps to relieve anxiety and depression.

- Garlic is a natural healer and an all-around tonic for your body.

- Brewer's yeast helps to relieve stress and fatigue.

- A high-protein breakfast will help boost your brain's production of dopamine, the neurotransmitter that creates a feeling of alertness, well-being, and happiness. Foods that act as building blocks for dopamine include apples, cucumber, sweet peppers, cheese, tofu, and watermelon.

HOME SPA TREATMENTS AND ACTIVITIES

Now that you've got your home spa set up, you're ready to try some soothing, energizing treatments.

Water Therapy

A great way to implement your home spa program is to take a long, hot bath. A shower feels good as well, but immersing your body in water causes your weight to be displaced, helping you to feel lighter and more buoyant, and therefore more at ease. The warm water promotes health, wellness, spiritual centeredness, and calmness, lowering your blood pressure and slowing your respiration. Water is a gentle healer.

If you wish, add a few drops of essential oil to your warm bathwater. Soak in your bath for at least twenty minutes, or until your muscles are completely relaxed. Imagine that you are switching off any negative thoughts and self-doubt and quieting the inner critic's nagging voice. Allow yourself to tend to your mind, body, and soul.

Movement Therapy

If you're feeling really stressed out and don't think you can relax in a hot bath, you might need some physical activity to help you switch off the negative messages and images in your mind. Yoga, tai chi, and Pilates are perfect ways to unwind and bring your body and mind together. If you can't find a class in any of these exercise practices, you can always purchase a DVD or videotape and try it at home. These movement forms can bring balance to your life and strength to your body, helping you to feel calmer. And when you're calm, you're happier, healthier, more productive, and better able to focus on your strengths for ultimate confidence.

Imagery is often used in yoga, tai chi, and Pilates. Here are two simple yoga stretching exercises, with names that will call to mind specific imagery.

A stretching cat. Get on all fours, like a cat, with your hands below your shoulders and your knees below your hips. Imagine a cat arching its back. Keeping this image in your mind, arch your back gently and drop your head down so that you are stretching from your neck to your "tail." Now, raise your head and let your back drop down toward the floor. Finally, return your head and back to a neutral position.

A roaring lion. Sit back on your heels with your feet tucked under your hips, or with your feet placed on the floor but with your weight shifted back toward the heels, whichever is comfortable for you. Place your hands on your thighs. Open your mouth as wide as you can to imitate a lion's roar, and stick out your tongue, stretching it as far as you can. This exercise will help you stretch your face and neck muscles.

CELEBRATING YOURSELF BUILDS CONFIDENCE

Doing good things for yourself will help you revitalize and celebrate yourself and all your strengths. You're worth it.

Now, let's try an exercise that you can use each and every morning to build upon your signature strengths and start the day off right, full of confidence and healthy self-esteem.

Awareness Exercise #16

1. Before getting out of bed, allow yourself to imagine how you'd like the day to go, feeling full of confidence, relaxed, and focused on your strengths. Imagine the best possible outcome for you and all the people you will encounter.

2. While still in bed, take a big, deep breath to fill your lungs with air, and stretch your body. If you had any dreams the night before, write them down. I always keep a small notebook on my nightstand so I can record the previous night's dreams. I find that the images in dreams are often potent indications of what's coming in the day ahead, or important messages about whatever may have been on my mind the day before. See yourself relaxed, happy, making a contribution to your world, and having a very positive day.

3. Now, it's time to get out of bed and get ready for the day. While you're getting dressed and eating breakfast, avoid listening to the television or radio news. Sing in the shower or listen to your favorite soothing or upbeat music to start your day off well.

4. Looking into the mirror, gaze with your left eye into your right eye to awaken the creative right side of your brain. Then switch your focus to the center of your forehead, between your eyebrows. Gaze intently at this spot for five to ten seconds and imagine your third eye, or inner eye, opening, revealing insight and foresight about your day.

5. While gazing at your face in the mirror, use your affirmations and tell yourself, "I'm strong and confident."

The Big Picture

Focus on the positive aspects of your life. When you focus on what's right and not what's wrong, you're setting yourself up for success and confidence. Don't focus on what you can't do. Instead, focus on what you can do, and then build from there. Your signature strengths are golden riches that no one can take away from you. They're what make you the unique individual you are. You are the author and authority in your own life. Allow yourself to feel good, and use self-care to nurture your body, mind, and spirit. Remind yourself that it's okay to add a little luxury to your life, and imagine yourself strong and confident each and every morning before you start your day.

Isn't it wonderful to feel strong, self-assured, and confident? After all, you're worth it and you deserve all good things coming to you. You're now living confidently!

8

living confidently

"Confidence is going after Moby Dick in a rowboat and taking the tartar sauce with you." —Zig Ziglar

Living confidently doesn't mean being arrogant, aggressive, or cocky. It simply means that you believe you can achieve your goals, you've mentally rehearsed each and every step in the process, you're solid in your strengths, and you're focused on a positive outcome. This can-do approach affects your attitudes and behavior, as well as the images and thoughts in your mind. You're now ready, willing, and able to be the best you can be.

Putting It All Together

You've now learned all the tools and techniques for living your life with self-confidence. Over the course of this book, you've identified your inner critic; you know where it comes from and how to stop it cold, instead of the other way around. You've learned that the inner critic, originally a protective mechanism, wants you to forget everything and run, or accept the falsehoods it puts forward. But you now know that you don't need to obey your inner critic. You've become aware that the messages and images the inner critic produces in your mind are false. With this new awareness, when the inner critic shows up in your life, you can appraise the situation, shift your perspective to the positive, and focus on what's right instead of what's wrong. You've discovered that your imagination makes you able to think outside the box, and, in doing so, you've dramatically built up your self-confidence, self-esteem, and feelings of personal power.

You've got what it takes. By discovering or rediscovering your golden nuggets of strength, you've aligned your ABCs of confidence (your attitudes, behaviors, and cognitions) in order to maximize your authentic potential. With the daily practice of guided imagery, you've learned to relax, quieting the body, mind, and spirit so you can center yourself before setting out to accomplish your goals. You've recognized that with repeated practice, mental rehearsal, and the aid of guided imagery, you can indeed live more dynamically.

You now recognize what real confidence is and what it isn't. You understand that your personal style of confidence is as unique as your own fingerprint. You appreciate that your inner confidence coach and your personal board of directors are available to you at any time and any place, for any confidence challenge you might face.

You've chosen what to focus on and you've created a personal vision board that clearly establishes what confidence looks like to you. Charting your progress using incremental benchmarks, you've begun to take "baby steps, baby steps, baby steps" toward your ultimate goal.

You're now committed to living a life of confidence. You embrace your authenticity, your ability to be autonomous, and your capacity to be the author of your own life. When you practice self-care, you know you're not being selfish—you're merely reinforcing in your mind that you are worthy of confidence and success. You've accomplished a lot since beginning this book! Congratulate yourself on a job well done. You did it!

Now, let's see how the experience of one person, utilizing all the techniques and exercises outlined in this book, became a confidence success story. Cheryl's story is inspiring, just as your life story is also full of hope, strength, and confidence. Cheryl followed this program faithfully and in doing so she had unexpected results: her most cherished dreams came true.

A Confidence Success Story: A First-Time Bride at Age Forty-Seven

For many years, Cheryl frequently compared herself to others. Whenever she did so, she always came up short. She felt that because she wasn't as far along in life or as successful as others there was something wrong with her, or that she had somehow missed the boat. She felt that she lacked the skills to better her life and felt stuck. She didn't feel she was progressing. In working with Cheryl, I suggested she consider the idea that she hadn't really missed the boat but was merely standing on the wrong pier. This image helped her understand that she was leading her life based upon the imagery of others, and that she focused on other people's expectations in order to measure her own self-worth. When Cheryl took the focus off others and placed it squarely on herself, amazing things began to happen in her life. Cheryl decided to set a goal for herself: to live confidently, without apologizing for who she was, and to be present in the world.

CHERYL'S INNER CRITIC AND INNER CONFIDENCE COACH

Cheryl identified her inner critic as a "big cloud filled with tension and obsessiveness" named Sister Fret. Sister Fret wouldn't allow Cheryl to focus on her many positive qualities. Instead, she caused Cheryl to worry and ruminate that she wasn't doing all she should be doing and led her to constantly compare herself to others.

Cheryl's inner confidence coach was Cinderella. Cheryl told me, "As a young girl I loved anything to do with Disneyland; it meant that dreams could and do come true. Cinderella is conscientious and pays attention to details. She is a nurturer." "These characteristics allow her to take care of others along the way, but they prevent her from tending to her own needs adequately. But she has a spirit about her: a playful spirit, a hopeful spirit. So, in the midst of cleaning in the dungeon while wearing old clothes, she sees herself living in a brighter way. As long as she wears torn rags she basically goes unnoticed. But when she puts on beautiful clothes with lots of color, she is transformed and noticed by the world. Fortunately for her, her prince has been waiting all along. He can see that she's had tough times, and he longs to care for her and tend to her innermost dreams."

FOCUSING ON HER ABCS

When Cheryl chose to focus on Cinderella, she understood what a kind, loving, and supportive figure she was. As she did, Cinderella helped Cheryl align her ABCs of confidence and learn to be true to her vision of a better future. Cheryl said, "Cinderella helps me fully embrace who I am. I don't worry about fitting in anymore and it's okay that my path hasn't been a straight one." "It's okay that my prince didn't really show up until I was forty-seven. My path has taught me to reinvent myself when necessary, and to use healthy self-talk to quiet Sister Fret. I still cut out pictures from magazines and place them on my vision board when they speak to me. When I do this, it helps me clarify my vision of hope, authenticity, autonomy, and abundance. The circumstances and pain I've encountered along the way while trying to fit into somebody else's idea of who I should be are now gone. I have the confidence to live my life and be true to my own self. I know that dreams do come true! If it happened for me, it can happen for others."

CHERYL'S VISION BOARD

The title of Cheryl's vision board was "Beginning to Be." It had large circles of friends and family all giving thanks. In her vision board Cheryl had also placed many images representing nature, travel, dancing, and walking on the beach with a significant other (although at the time she was single). For Cheryl, creating a vision board was "the first time that my life's path made any sense. Prior to doing this exercise, my life had always seemed so fragmented and I wasn't able to explain it to anyone. Therefore, I often wouldn't receive any validation, and consequently, this affected my self-esteem. I couldn't focus on the positive. I thought I was doing everything all wrong and I always grieved about the life I didn't have. Framing the pieces of my life together on a vision board provided me clarity and allowed me to present my authentic self to the world. When I did this, I received validation. I became the author of my life, and I began to be the person I always wanted to be."

BABY STEPS, BABY STEPS, BABY STEPS

With Cinderella, her inner confidence coach, by her side to keep her on the path toward strong confidence, healthy self-esteem, and belief in her positive qualities, Cheryl began to see some dramatic changes in her life. Her sense of abundance grew, and "good friends who believed in me encouraged me to take baby steps toward my confidence goals. I was actually beginning to be the real me!"

Cheryl maintained a focus on her vision, stayed positive, and took daily incremental steps. "I kept viewing the pictures on my vision board. They gave me an image to see in my mind even when things didn't look good, especially when I was in very toxic work environments. I wrote down the things I wanted and pasted them on the bathroom mirror and refrigerator doors."

BIG IMPACTS FROM SMALL CHANGES, AND A NEW LIFE

Cheryl kept practicing each and every day. She placed her vision board in a spot in her bedroom where she could see it early in the morning and late at night. She practiced good self-care, took one step at a time, listened to the wise and supportive voice of her inner confidence coach, and continued working on her program. Meanwhile, Robert, an old boyfriend whom she had not seen for many years, came back into her life, and they slowly rekindled their romance. One day Cheryl invited me to lunch and began showing me photographs of bridal outfits. With a light in her eyes and a smile on her face, Cheryl told me that she was going to be a first-time bride at the age of forty-seven. Even though life had sent these two down separate paths, they were now reunited and were looking forward to spending the rest of their lives together. Talk about big impacts!

Several months later I witnessed Cheryl and Robert exchanging vows on a clear, sunny Southern California morning. It was clear to all who knew her that she had focused on her signature strengths, embraced her own authenticity and her own counsel, and truly created a storybook chapter in her life. Beaming with joy, Cheryl walked down the aisle, confident, relaxed, and present in the world for all to see.

The minister who married Cheryl and Robert began by saying, "The day has come. Not a day too soon. Not a day too late. Today is the perfect day." What a wonderful way to sum up Cheryl's journey toward self-confidence and self-determination—she did it her own way, at her own speed, and when she was ready, she arrived, triumphantly, at the place she was meant to be.

It Can Happen for You Too

Just like Cheryl, you're not stuck unless you believe yourself to be stuck. You don't lack self-confidence unless you believe it to be true. When you take the focus off of others and don't compare yourself to everyone else around you, you stop beating yourself up. Instead, you place your focus squarely back on yourself, and you reinforce your natural feelings of abundance. You appreciate your own golden nuggets of strength. As surely as it did for Cheryl, your day will come—not a minute too soon, not a minute too late, but at the perfect time and place.

PRESENTING THE NEW YOU TO THE WORLD

From this moment on, imagine yourself as a brilliant diamond or other precious jewel. Begin to see your life as a work of art. Together with your creative imagination, you are the cocreator of your life. As your inner world of imagery, sensations, attitudes, emotions, and thoughts expands you'll see a corresponding expansion of your energy in the world. With everyone you meet you'll be spreading your own light and empowerment. This creative process will continue throughout your life; you'll be a work of art that becomes more powerful, more inspiring, and more beautiful the more the artist (you) continues to work with it.

For centuries men and women have used their imaginations to think creatively, solve problems, enhance their health, and develop confidence to make a difference in the world. Over the next several weeks and months, return to the imagery scripts in this book as often as you want or need to. Experiment with them, and allow yourself to get to know the imagery that comes to you in as many forms as possible. Remember, your inner confidence coach is with you at all times; this inner wisdom doesn't depend on any outside influences. You don't have to go someplace special, or have an extreme external makeover. All that's required is willingness and consistent practice to unlock and tap into the vast reservoir of your imagination.

Continue to use guided imagery to overcome unhelpful habits, change your moods, explore your emotions, rehearse before entering challenging situations, and connect with your inner confidence coach for encouragement and support when you most need it. As you turn your insights into action, you'll discover yourself finding greater purpose and meaning to your life. As you begin to live confidently, imagine the following:

- Strength

- Courage

- Conviction

- Happiness

- Success

- Love

- Prosperity

- Assurance

- Health

- Peace

- Joy

Practical Reminders for Living Confidently

Let's put it all together with some practical and simple reminders to help you stay balanced, focused, and on target:

- Visualize the outcome you are seeking. Be clear and specific; every day, imagine yourself with the feelings, sensations, and attitudes that go along with your desired outcome as if you have already achieved that goal. Fake it 'til you make it.

- Quiet your mind and body daily.

- Trust your intuition.

- What you believe is what you get.

- Be willing.

- Take action. Any action, no matter how small, in the right direction will keep you on target.

- Give yourself interim benchmarks. Allow yourself to take incremental baby steps toward your goal. Fix, eliminate, add, or change your benchmarks periodically.

- Chart your progress.

- Let your imagination soar. Be willing to stretch, to try and try again.

- Don't hold back. Go for it.

Nicholas Lore, in his book, *The Pathfinder*, says that "whether it be an artistic work, a scientific breakthrough, or a new way to do business, true creativity … creates new, previously unimagined pathways and possibilities" (1998, 258). Using imagery is the perfect way to tap into your inner creativity in order to reinvent yourself. It's this ability to reinvent yourself that is one of the most extraordinary of human aptitudes. As Lore writes, "you may not be an Einstein or a Picasso, but you have an untapped reservoir of this most extraordinary ability. … You can be the author of your life."

Each and Every Day and Night

Every night, close your eyes and take a few moments to review your day. Run through your actions and responses in your mind. How did your morning go? The afternoon? What do you wish you had done differently? What obstacles got in your way? What resources did you call upon? What surprised you? Make a mental note to yourself about what went well, and what might need some more attention and focus. Use this technique over and over again until it becomes second nature to you and a regular part of your day and evening ritual.

Additionally, take a few moments every morning to do the following awareness exercises.

Awareness Exercise #17

Look at your vision board. Start a new page in your notebook, and complete the sentences below:

Today, I will _____.

Today, I can _____.

Today, I am _____.

Finally, each morning and evening, practice saying—and believing—the confidence affirmations in the following exercise.

Awareness Exercise #18

Write the following affirmations down on paper and tape them to your mirror, scribble them on sticky notes and place them on your refrigerator door, or write them on index cards and carry them around in your pocket. Whatever method you choose, allow images that reinforce the affirmations to come into your mind as you say them.

I expect the best and it comes to me.

My confidence is growing daily.

I can achieve my heart's desire.

I'm in the right place at the right time.

I know exactly what to say.

I am at ease with everyone I meet.

I now see life as a journey filled with wonder.

I now go with the flow; life is a joy.

The best is yet to be.

Timeless Words of Wisdom

Thomas Jefferson wrote, "Nothing can stop the man with the right mental attitude from achieving his goal; nothing on earth can help the man with the wrong attitude." Develop a can-do attitude. You can achieve your goals.

Frederick Langbridge wrote, "Two men look out the same prison bars; one sees mud and the other sees stars." When you look at your life, how do you view it? Are you focusing on the mud, or do you see the stars? Try to see the stars.

The ancient Greek philosopher Epictetus wrote, "It's not what happens to you, but how you react to it that matters." Use guided imagery to practice new ways of reacting and acting.

Buddha taught, "We are what we think. All that we are arises with our thoughts. With our thoughts we make the world." With your guided imagery practice, be what you think.

Gandhi said, "Be the change you wish to see in the world." In order to live a life of confidence, be confident. Believe it.

Mark Twain said, "Keep away from people who try to belittle your ambitions. Small people always do that, but the really great make you feel that you, too, can become great." Surround yourself with truly great people. Your board of directors and your confidence coach will inspire you to greatness.

Babe Ruth said, "Don't let fear of striking out hold you back." When it's your turn at bat, don't let fear hold you back. Go for a grand slam.

Being Confident

You are the producer, screenwriter, star, and director of your own life. As we come to the end of this book, let's use one last guided imagery script to anchor into your consciousness all that you have accomplished up until this point. Allow your creative imagination to enjoy this exercise and know that confidence is yours.

Guided Imagery Exercise #9

1. *You are now going to imagine that your life has been made into a highly successful movie. Don't be so surprised. It happened to Erin Brockovich, a seemingly ordinary person, and she was portrayed by Julia Roberts! The same thing happened to Sister Helen Prejean, whose fierce love and loyalty were dramatized by Susan Sarandon in* Dead Man Walking, *and to Oskar Schindler when he was portrayed by Liam Neeson in* Schindler's List. *Consider also labor organizer Crystal Lee Sutton's heroism as dramatized by Sally Field in* Norma Rae, *or astronaut Jim Lovell's bravery as performed by Tom Hanks in* Apollo 13. *The point of this exercise is to let your imagination fly and dream that you too can be bigger than life.*

2. *You're now very comfortable with how to enter a state of deep relaxation to calm your mind and body. Gently close your eyes, and allow your breathing to soften as you relax deeply using the now-familiar script. When you are deeply relaxed, allow yourself to imagine the following scenes.*

3. *You're sitting comfortably in a reclining seat in an elegant movie theater. The lights dim, the deep-red velvet curtains open, and your life begins to unfold on the screen.*

4. *You see the most moving and important scenes of your life playing out on the screen. Notice who is playing you in the movie of your life. What actors play the other significant people in your life? What time of day is it in the scenes you are watching? What are you wearing? Where are you?*

5. *As the movie of your life plays out, imagine yourself confident, strong, and powerful.*
    What is the title of the movie?

6. *Now, let this image of your life on the screen fade and allow your focus to shift to Oscar night. Picture yourself walking down the red carpet at the Academy Awards, beautifully dressed in a stunning gown or an elegant tuxedo. Photographers snap your picture and reporters ask you to stop and chat. You enter the theater, and you're now sitting in the audience. All around you excitement is brewing.*

7. *The time comes for the award for outstanding actor or actress. All eyes are on the presenter, who is reading the names of the nominees. And, lo and behold, instead of calling out the name of the winning actor or actress, the presenter calls your name. You've won an Oscar for being you! Imagine your excitement. You gracefully rise from your seat and make your way to the stage.*

8. *You're feeling confident and exhilarated at being recognized for simply being yourself. Now up on the stage, you hold out your arms and accept your golden statue. You approach the microphone. What do you say? Whom do you thank? Hear the applause. Feel the room and imagine this wonderful moment with great intensity. Enjoy the pleasant feelings that come with a job well done.*

9. *When you know the time is right, allow all these images to fade and, using the same ending script you've used many times before, begin to bring your awareness back into your body. Wiggle your toes and fingers and gradually, slowly, open your eyes.*

10. *When you're fully alert, take some time to reflect about your movie life and write about it in your journal. You are the star of your life. You have always had the power to create the moving pictures in your mind. By being optimistic, focusing on positive imagery, and taking small daily steps, you have made your dreams of confidence come true.*

The Big Picture

This has been an incredible journey. You've come full circle. Using guided imagery, you've gained new insight about your life. Your new insight propelled you to new self-knowledge and appreciation of who you are. This new awareness and knowledge have formed the basis for positive growth. Your new insights have led you to new perceptions, and these new perceptions have in turn encouraged you to take new actions, using mental rehearsals along the way. Your new actions have resulted in new behaviors, new ways of thinking and being. With your new insights, perceptions, attitudes, and behavior, you've explored new options, both in your imagination and in your real life, which have opened up a new world for you. A world of confidence.

You have all the guided imagery tools and techniques you'll ever need to visualize confidence and overcome self-doubt.

Believe it. Know it.

You're worth it. I know you can do it.

I wish you all the success and confidence in the world.

Remember, it all begins with an image in your mind—an image that is truly worth a thousand words.

resources

In addition to the many books and articles listed in the References section, below are several suggested books that you may find useful as you continue to develop your self-confidence. You'll also find some books that explore guided imagery, and some Web site addresses to check out in order to learn more.

Books

Achterberg, Jeanne. 2002. *Imagery in Healing: Shamanism and Modern Medicine*. Boston: Shambala Publications.

Cameron, Julia. 2002. *The Artist's Way: A Spiritual Path to Higher Creativity*. New York: Jeremy P. Tarcher/Putnam.

Epstein, Gerald. 1989. *Healing Visualizations: Creating Health Through Imagery*. New York: Bantam.

Gawain, Shatki. 2002. *Creative Visualization: Use the Power of Your Imagination to Create What You Want in Your Life*. Novato, CA: New World Library.

Hudson, Frederic M., and Pamela McLean. 2000. *Life Launch: A Passionate Guide to the Rest of Your Life*. 3rd ed. Santa Barbara, CA: Hudson Institute Press.

Jeffers, Susan. 1988. *Feel the Fear and Do It Anyway*. New York: Ballantine Books.

McKay, M., P. Fanning, C. Honeychurch, and C. Sutker. 1999. *The Self-Esteem Companion: Simple Exercises to Help You Challenge Your Inner Critic and Celebrate Your Personal Strengths.* Oakland, CA: New Harbinger Publications.

Rossman, M. L. 2004. Guided imagery in cancer care. *Seminars in Integrative Medicine* 2(3):99–106.

Samuels, Michael. 2003. *Healing with the Mind's Eye: How to Use Guided Imagery and Visions to Heal Body, Mind, and Spirit.* Hoboken, NJ: John Wiley & Sons.

Samuels, M., and N. Samuels. 1975. *Seeing with the Mind's Eye.* New York: Random House.

Web Sites

The following Web sites are excellent resources for learning more about guided imagery.

www.academyforguidedimagery.com

This site contains excellent information on the Academy for Guided Imagery, cofounded by David Bresler, Ph.D., and Martin Rossman, MD, and its certification program in Interactive Guided Imagery. It also contains up-to-date research findings.

www.drweil.com

Andrew Weil, MD, is internationally recognized as a pioneer in integrative medicine, including guided imagery.

www.healthjourneys.com

Belleruth Naparstek, LISW, another leader in the field of guided imagery as well as a dedicated psychotherapist, popular author, and lecturer, offers this Web site.

www.thehealingmind.org

The Web site for Martin Rossman, MD, is another excellent source of additional information, books, and audiotapes.

references

Aanstoos, C., I. Serlin, and T. Greening. 2000. History of Division 32: Humanistic Psychology. In *Unification Through Division: Histories of the Divisions of the American Psychological Association*. Vol. 5, ed. D. Dewsbury, Washington, DC: American Psychological Association.

Achterberg, J., B. Dossey, and L. Kolkmeier. 1994. *Rituals of Healing: Using Imagery for Health and Wellness*. New York: Bantam Books.

Aron, E. 1997. *The Highly Sensitive Person*. New York: Broadway.

Brantley, J., and W. Millstine. 2005. *Five Good Minutes: 100 Morning Practices to Help You Stay Calm and Focused All Day Long*. Oakland, CA: New Harbinger Publications.

Bresler, D., and M. L. Rossman. 2004. *Fundamentals of Interactive Guided Imagery: Essential Training in Mind/Body Communication for Health Care Professionals*. Malibu, CA: Awareness Press and Academy for Guided Imagery.

Covey, S. 2004. *The 7 Habits of Highly Effective People*. New York: Free Press.

Csikszentmihalyi, M. 1991. *Flow: The Psychology of Optimal Experience*. New York: Harper Perennial.

————. 1997. *Creativity: Flow and the Psychology of Discovery and Invention*. New York: Harper Perennial.

DeRoo, C., and C. DeRoo. 2006. *What's Right with Me: Positive Ways to Celebrate Your Strengths, Build Self-Esteem, and Reach Your Potential.* Oakland, CA: New Harbinger Publications.

Dyer, W. W. 2001. *You'll See It When You Believe It: The Way to Your Personal Transformation.* New York: Quill Publications.

Gawain, S. 1978. *Creative Visualization: Use the Power of Your Imagination to Create What You Want in Your Life.* Berkeley, CA: Whatever Publications.

———. 2002. *Creative Visualization: Use the Power of Your Imagination to Create What You Want in Your Life.* Novato, CA: New World Library.

Hall, J. C. 2002. Imagery practice and the development of surgical skills. *American Journal of Surgery.* 184:465–70.

Harkness, H. 1997. *The Career Chase: Taking Creative Control in a Chaotic Age.* Palo Alto, CA: Davies-Black Publishing.

Lore, N. 1998. *The Pathfinder: How to Choose or Change Your Career for a Lifetime of Satisfaction and Success.* New York: Fireside.

Maurer, R. 2004. *One Small Step Can Change Your Life: The Kaizen Way.* New York: Workman Publishing Company.

McKay, M., and P. Fanning. 2000. *Self-Esteem: A Proven Program of Cognitive Techniques for Assessing, Improving, and Maintaining Your Self-Esteem.* Oakland, CA: New Harbinger Publications.

Merriam-Webster. 2003. *Merriam-Webster's Collegiate Dictionary.* Springfield, MA: Merriam-Webster.

Murray, W. H. 1951. *The Scottish Himalayan Expedition.* London: J. M. Dent & Sons, Ltd.

Perkins-Reed, M. 1996. *Thriving in Transition: Effective Living in Times of Change*. New York: Touchstone.

Rockefeller, K. 1993. Psychoneuroimmunology and biopsychosocial cofactors of HIV-spectrum disease and long-term survivors. Doctoral candidacy essay, Saybrook Graduate School and Research Center, San Francisco.

Rossman, M. L. 2000. *Guided Imagery for Self-Healing: An Essential Resource for Anyone Seeking Wellness*. Tiburon, CA: H. J. Kramer/New World Library.

————. 2003. *Fighting Cancer from Within: How to Use the Power of Your Mind for Healing*. New York: Henry Holt and Company.

Seligman, M. E. 1998. *Learned Optimism: How to Change Your Mind and Your Life*. New York: Free Press.

————. 2002. *Authentic Happiness: Using the New Positive Psychology to Realize Your Potential for Lasting Fulfillment*. New York: Free Press.

Seligman, M. E., and M. Csikszentmihalyi. 2000. Positive psychology: An introduction. *American Psychologist* 55(1):5–14.

Shakespeare, W. 1980. *The Complete Works of Shakespeare*. 3rd ed. Edited by D. Bevington. Glenview, IL: Scott, Foresman and Company.

Sperry, R. W., E. Zaidel, and D. Zaidel. 1979. Self recognition and social awareness in the deconnected minor hemisphere. *Neuropsychologia* 17:153–66.

Stone, H., and S. Stone. 1993. *Embracing Your Inner Critic: Turning Self-Criticism into a Creative Asset*. San Francisco: HarperSanFrancisco.

Williamson, M. 1996. *A Return to Love: Reflections on the Principles of a Course in Miracles*. New York: HarperCollins.

Zubieta, J. K., J. A. Bueller, L. R. Jackson, D. J. Scott, Y. Xu, R. A. Koeppe, T. E. Nichols, et al. 2005. Placebo effects mediated by endogenous opioid activity on μ-opioid receptors. *Journal of Neuroscience* 25(34):7754–62.

Photo by Doug Gifford

Kirwan Rockefeller, Ph.D., is the director of arts and humanities continuing education at the University of California, Irvine. His expertise includes psychology, visual and performing arts, humanities, and body-mind modalities. He has consulted with top national and entertainment organizations on the accurate depiction of social and mental health issues including the Entertainment Industries Council, Centers for Disease Control and Prevention, National Institute on Drug Abuse, The Robert Wood Johnson Foundation, and Ogilvy Public Relations Worldwide, in addition to teaching organizational behavior and social psychology at the doctoral level. He is coeditor of *Psychology, Spirituality and Healthcare,* Volume 2 of *Mind-Body Medicine: The Art of Whole Person Healthcare.* He is a member of the American and California Psychological Associations and lives in Newport Beach, CA. (www.kirwanrockefeller.com)

more **titles for becoming a better you**
from new**harbinger**publications

FIVE GOOD MINUTES™
100 Morning Practices to Help You Stay Calm
& Focused All Day Long
$14.95 • Item Code: 4143

WHAT'S RIGHT WITH ME
Positive Ways to Celebrate Your Strengths,
Build Self-Esteem & Reach Your Potential
$16.95 • Item Code: 4429

**HOW TO STOP BACKING DOWN
& START TALKING BACK**

$13.95 • Item Code: 4178

THE MEMORY DOCTOR
Fun, Simple Techniques to Improve
Memory & Boost Your Brain Power
$11.95 • Item Code: 3708

GET OUT OF YOUR MIND & INTO YOUR LIFE
The New Acceptance & Commitment Therapy
$19.95 • Item Code: 4259

available from new**harbinger**publications
and fine booksellers everywhere

To order, call toll free **1-800-748-6273** or visit our online bookstore at **www.newharbinger.com**
(V, MC, AMEX • prices subject to change without notice)